Signs *of* Hope

Recognizing Messages
from the Afterlife

Ellen Matthews Oetinger

FIRST EDITION
Wings on Fox Publishing

ISBN: 978-1-7358822-0-8 *(Paperback)*

Cover Design by 100covers.com
Cover Art by Rosalie Phipps
Interior Design by FormattedBooks.com

DEDICATION

For Dad, 'til we meet again

CONTENTS

PROLOGUE

Upon walking into the room, I found him wild eyed, his chest heaving as he tried to catch his breath. Pulling up a chair next to him, I thought about what to do first. I said as calmly as possible, "I'm here. It's going to be OK. I need for you to try to slow down your breathing a bit. Come on, we'll do this together."

He stared at me in sort of a daze while seemingly unable to control his breathing, his whole body racked with tension; his fear palpable. I watched his ultimate nightmare playing out in real life. Knowing his history of claustrophobia, I had to get him to slow his breathing down. His panic would only increase his anxiety which could mean real trouble!

Trying to push aside my own fear, I began demonstrating to him on how to get better control of his breathing. "OK, let's do this together. Come on, follow my lead—big breath in, breathe out—like this." I showed him how to take a big intake of air as controlled as possible and then exhale through pursed lips. I couldn't help but think, "We're going to be in big trouble soon if he can't get it under control. I continued my mantra: "Big breath in, breathe out slowly, big breath in, breathe out slowly." I tried sorting out all the possibilities that could happen if this scenario worsened, most of them terrifying me.

With no time to let up, I laid my right hand on his forearm to offer some meager form of comfort and ignored the fact that he was barely dressed. The minutes slowly ticked off. Together we continued our breathing while I attempted to get him to follow my lead. "Let's try to slow it down a bit more. You can do this, OK? Big breath in (my own lungs filled with air), now, slowly, let it out" (I exhaled with him as slowly as possible).

"How much longer can he endure this?" I wondered.

Tears of frustration came to my eyes seeing this man suffer. To add to my confusion and feelings of hopelessness, I had intense feelings of dislike for him. It just seemed unbelievable that circumstances put us together in this horrible situation, and frankly, this whole event seemed downright unfair.

More than once that night, I looked up to God saying, "Really God? Really? Why me? Please tell me what to do?"

And through all my fear and exasperation, He answered.

INTRODUCTION

"Mom, no one wants to hear that much about you," my 26-year-old son, Henrik, said after I read to him the second attempt of the beginning of this book. "People want to read about your signs," he continued, being especially nice because he knows how sensitive his mother can be. Trying to keep my composure, I countered, "But, Henrik, I can't jump into trying to explain how all these signs began. It's important to illustrate I'm just an ordinary person. There is nothing special about me to explain why these uncanny signs made their appearance. If this all happened to me, the same can surely happen to anyone." Henrik remained quiet as I continued in my defense. "A little backstory seems important before illustrating why an ordinary clock, a late model Ford, a cell phone, a moth that seemingly could appear and disappear at will, and all the other weird things I witnessed can actually prove noteworthy enough to provide a basis for a book."

"Alright, Mom, I get it. But please, don't overdo it." My son is fully aware of my family's history of "Go Big or Go Home" and how I can maybe get a bit carried away with my storytelling. Bearing this in mind, I proceed with literary caution.

So, before jumping in to explain why a series of random coincidences has given me the nickname of "The Sign Seer" by my sons and husband, let me provide a bit of information leading up to when these unusual events first began.

I am a woman fortunate enough to grow up in my preteen years in a "Mayberry" kind of town called Shelbyville, Kentucky (population roughly 5,000 in 1970). I lived on a real-life "All American" Main Street in the "Big White House." I was one of four children and my family resembled a cross between the Cleavers from *Leave It to Beaver* and the Keatons from *Family Ties*. I'm old enough to remember wearing white gloves along with white (or black) patent leather shoes to Sunday School each week before fashions got a big makeover thanks to the advent of the women's lib movement in the early '70s. After my eighth birthday, I had permission to walk or ride my bicycle anywhere within the town limits I desired. Unlike nowadays with children's lives scheduled to the minute, I'm pretty sure my mother never truly knew where any of her children were between break-fast and dinner. We were, however, expected to be home in time for the evening meal we always shared together as a family.

Raised fiercely independent, I was encouraged by my parents and grandmother to be almost anything I wanted to be. I thought about becoming an English teacher; however, in the early 1980s teachers were poorly paid in Kentucky. Fearing I would have to permanently live at home because I couldn't support myself, I turned to a different career option. This one appeared to offer greater pay and would allow me to move anywhere in the country I desired.

Nursing.

My decision didn't entirely win over all my family members. When I told my grandmother (we affectionately called her Mimi) I had enrolled in nursing school after my second year in college, she tearfully said, "You'll spend your life scrubbing floors and washing sheets." Having been born in 1902, she had fixed ideas of what nurses were still doing 80 years later.

After graduation, I excitedly began my career in 1985 working night shifts on a floor taking care of patients who suffered from mostly respiratory ailments. Because the hospital is located in tobacco-loving bluegrass country, we stayed busy. Ironically at the time, many nurses and physicians were smoking as much as our patients were *inside* the hospital in our lounge located mere feet from patient rooms.

Nursing provided a means to support myself until I achieved my real dream job: becoming a wife and mother (television shows of my childhood made motherhood appear so easy and fun). The biggest obstacle so far to reaching my goal was finding a suitable "beau" (the term Mimi used to refer to all of the men I dated).

One year exactly after I began my nursing career, fate interrupted my half-hearted plan to become a mobile nurse and "see the world." A last-minute decision to attend a party changed my life instantly when I met a tall, somewhat dark, and handsome guy named Pete. He first impressed me with his pick-up line, "I'll give you twenty dollars if you can spell my last name correctly." I didn't get the twenty bucks but I ended up getting the last name. Upon meeting each other, we became inseparable. After six months of dating, he asked me on Christmas Eve, "Will you marry me? But not for another year and a half because we don't know each other that well." Feeling desperately in love with him and maybe a bit afraid because, at the age of 23, I might not get another proposal, I quickly answered, "Yes, I will marry you, *but* it will be within the year." Sure enough, Pete and I were married ten months later with all the proverbial bells and whistles.

And now, unbelievably, it is the summer of 2020. Pete and I have been married for almost 33 years. Our two grown sons moved away long ago. Along with most of our friends, we nervously contemplate our future thanks to a recent pandemic fueled by a new Coronavirus. The appearance of this deadly "bug" has literally upset most everyone's feelings of well-being along with the ability to leave the house without great concern—and a mask.

I suddenly found myself furloughed from one of my part-time jobs. Pete and I viewed taking a trip to the grocery as a possibly dangerous expedition, so we went as little as possible. Only a few days into the isolation, I already felt bored.

But a few good things have come out of the "Stay at Home" order that went into effect for people living in my community on March 23rd lasting for several weeks.

Without any expectation, I received a phone call that changed everything for me and my enforced idleness. With new encouragement from a person whom I had only met once, I received a "calling" to finish writing the book I had started years before. This collection of stories is about a series of odd coincidences which happened to Pete and me personally over the previous 15 years. With so much bad news being reported on every type of medium, it suddenly seemed like a good time to share my "Signs of Hope" in an effort to counterbalance endless days clouded over by confusion, anxiety and fear caused by this mysterious new "Covid-19" virus.

The following true stories are accurate to the best of my memory. Names have been changed (denoted by an asterisk) to protect a person's privacy when necessary. They are purposefully kept in chronological order. Henrik suggested I place the most exciting "signs" at the beginning of the book. While his idea might make sense if this were written as a fictional thriller, instead I want you to read about them as they happened, in the order they happened. See for yourself how funny coincidences continued to occur to the point that I could no longer accept them as mere happenstance. Ordinary became extraordinary.

What makes them most unusual?

Well, for one thing, most all of these messages were sent from friends or relatives soon *after* they died. Yes, *after* they died. Secondly, they all happened to me or my husband personally. In the process of sharing my stories, other friends have shared an isolated event when they too felt they experienced a sign from a loved one. I just happen to be "lucky" enough to have experienced more than the apparent average.

If the following circumstances happened to you, would you recognize them as possible signs, coincidences, a "Godcidence," (a coincidence seemingly directed by God) or dismiss them entirely? How many instances would it take for you to start thinking something otherworldly might be happening?

CHAPTER 1

The Invitation

By 1999, my family and I had been living in bucolic Wallingford, Pennsylvania, a suburb of Philadelphia, for over two years. Having been out of the hospital workplace since my firstborn Phil arrived on a hot, muggy summer day in Houston, Texas, in 1990, I became more or less resigned to never working in the nursing field again. Phil (age 8) and Henrik (age 5) were keeping me busy as an at-home mom and I relished the time spent as homeroom mother and library aide. To escape from my house one night a week, I joined a local singing group, The Valley Voices. Being still new to the area with few good friends, I enjoyed attending the regular Thursday night rehearsals where I looked forward to the company of fellow singers.

One woman in particular, Mary Jo*, liked to chat a bit with me (even when we were supposed to be singing). Finding Mary Jo exceptionally friendly with a great sense of humor, I enjoyed talking with her despite our not having much in common. I knew little about her other than that she was a registered nurse who had worked in a psychiatric facility before recently retiring. Her work history impressed me. I had dabbled in all kinds of different fields of nursing: cardiac, plastic surgery, pulmonary, community out-reach, but psychiatric nursing? With great certainty, I can say that this particular type of nursing had never appealed to me. Actually, the field still scares the willies out of me. Apparently not having much of a knack for this particular branch of nursing, I barely got through my psych rotation during my ini-tial training.

One Thursday evening in early December 1998, Mary Jo asked if she could talk to me after rehearsal. "Sure," I told her, curious to know what she wanted to discuss.

It turns out Mary Jo had a job offer. She told me she worked private duty for a woman who lives in a comfortable but simply appointed apartment located in an exclusive assisted-living community about 30 minutes from my house. "We need another RN to work a couple of evenings a week," she explained. She made the job sound wonderful: easy hours, great pay, along with light duty nursing requirements. She gave me few details other than that the client I would be caring for had been in a psychiatric hospital for much of her adult life. Now, in her early 80's, she required less nursing supervision; instead, she only needed more or less good old companionship most octogenarians enjoy.

How could I say no? I felt more than qualified. I could be a decent "companion." Moving fast, I hurried to complete the paperwork for my Pennsylvania nursing license, the only formal requirement for the position.

Little did I know the job I began in April 1999 would have a profound impact on me and my family, and would ultimately lead to receiving my first sign, sent by a "reluctant" woman of faith who loved her life so much, she convinced herself she would never die. She sure had me convinced for many years.

I'll call this woman, my client for the next six years, Charlotte. Born in an affluent suburb of Cleveland, Ohio, Charlotte, the youngest of three children, grew up in a lifestyle befitting a princess. Her father reportedly made his fortune in lumber, railroads, and oil, or so I was told. Born healthy during the burgeoning Edwardian era, she enjoyed her toddler years living securely because of her father's great wealth. Unfortunately, money couldn't buy her continued good health.

Before Charlotte turned four (during the influenza pandemic of 1918), she became gravely ill with a bacterial infection. She survived the near-mortal illness, barely, but suffered permanent damage to the part of her brain that shapes and controls mood and personality. I was told that as she grew into her teen years, she became more and more afflicted by sudden violent outbursts, making it difficult for her to have normal relationships with family and friends. When the outbursts became more frequent and difficult to control, Charlotte had to be institutionalized. Charlotte's hospital became her permanent home for decades, with the staff nurses becoming her primary caregivers and second family.

She had already celebrated her 83rd birthday before our first meeting. With no case notes to read, I found her to be more or less an enigma for the longest time. I had patient information on a need-to-know basis, and apparently, I didn't need to know much. I learned a few things quickly. First and foremost, she enjoyed being pampered and getting her own way. She loved all food, absolutely adored music, and she enjoyed a variety of discussion topics–from travel to politics. She also enjoyed demonstrating her sharp mind by reciting verbatim poetry she had learned in her youth.

Having the means, she often paid her favorite nurses to accompany her on outings to lunch and dinner. On occasion, she treated some of the staff to expensive trips abroad as well as to many lovely resorts around the United States. Years of therapy and a boatload of medications kept her functioning well enough to get out and about on occasion, but she was never stable enough to live on her own. As she aged, she became totally dependent on the company of her "family" of nurses who happily spoiled Charlotte. She loved any and all attention given to her, finding it especially thrilling to actively participate in any special event or party. Of course, it also helped that Charlotte footed the bill for all expenses for most of these occasions.

The best term to describe Charlotte is "properly plain". She was not beautiful but yet, very attractive in her unique way. Though there wasn't one dramatic feature which stood out about her appearance, Charlotte did possess an amazing physical characteristic I noticed immediately upon meeting her. She had absolutely no lines or wrinkles between her eyes or on her forehead. In fact, she had the most unlined face for a woman of 83 years I had ever seen, all without the benefit of plastic surgery. Her beautiful skin seemed to be evidence of the protected, sheltered, and pampered life she enjoyed for most of her adult years, a tribute to the wonderful care she must have received for all those decades in the institution.

She ended up in her present beautiful "home" where I first met her as a result of harrowing circumstances. When asked, Mary Jo explained, "A couple of years ago another long-time nurse for Charlotte was taking her out to lunch. Some of us enjoyed this on a regular basis. We'd chauffeur Charlotte in our own cars usually parked right outside the hospital. On one particular afternoon, Judy* was opening the passenger door for Charlotte. Suddenly, despite it being in the middle of the day, they both heard the unmistakable sound of gunshots. 'Pop, Pop, Pop.' More frightening was the fact the shots sounded extremely close. Judy said this was the last straw for her. The neighborhood surrounding Charlotte's hospital had clearly become too unsafe to continue with the outings in the nurses' personal vehicles. Other nurses also expressed their fear of taking Charlotte out safely in their cars. Something needed to change."

Those ultimately in charge of Charlotte's well-being decided it would be best for Charlotte to be mainstreamed into living with people her age and with similar wealth. With money no object, Charlotte was soon moved to an exclusive continuing care facility complete with sprawling manicured grounds, deluxe apartments, a nursing unit, and best of all, a beautiful mansion where Charlotte could host social affairs. When I first took Charlotte for walks around the property, it was fun imagining what it must have been like to have lived on this beautiful estate in the 1920s, possibly hosting my own "Great Gatsby" type of parties.

When Charlotte moved to her new "home," over ten registered nurses with psychiatric experience were hired as private duty nursing "companions." They were primarily brought on to keep Charlotte company during her waking hours. When I came aboard, Charlotte had been in her new home for about a year. I had no idea what to do to help keep Charlotte company at first, but I soon learned she most definitely knew what my role was while in her employ.

Charlotte thrived on routine and I learned quickly to stick to it. Our evenings together were often scripted exactly the same. We ate dinner together shortly after my arrival. After dessert, we headed outside for a walk when the weather cooperated. If the facility sponsored an evening program, she expected to attend. After we returned to her room, I got busy helping her get settled in for the night. My list of duties included: helping her change into her night clothes after she picked out her outfit for the following day, administering her evening medications, washing out her support hose and hanging them to dry, lining up her supplies for oral care, and finally settling in with her for an hour or so of listening to music or watching television. She especially adored Rick Steves' shows detailing his travels from all over the world. Despite being hospitalized for many years, Charlotte had toured many major cities across several continents. She recalled her more recent vacations well.

I say the word "recall" loosely. Charlotte never shared any details of events that happened to her between the years of 1940 and 1985; however, she easily remembered every word to every popular song from 1930 to 1950 played during sing-a-long time. I knew better than to pry for details of her younger years. In fact, during the years I knew Charlotte, instinct told me to not ask many personal questions, period. She clearly wasn't interested in talking about her distant past. Instead, we found it great fun to attend every musical event the facility offered. I'd had a fair amount of singing experience with school and church choirs and we gaily sang along together familiar tunes such as, "You Are My Sunshine," "Amazing Grace" and "She'll Be Comin' Round the Mountain," and the timeless favorite, "This Land is Your Land." I think I had as much fun as Charlotte did while participating in the constant stream of activity her facility offered.

Our life together remained a constant for many months. At bedtime, while tucking her in under her fluffy down duvet, she always asked as if on cue, "Ellen, are you going to sing to me?"

"Of course, Charlotte," I'd respond (as if had much choice). And so, for the next few years, every evening when on duty before saying goodnight, I sang "The Lord's Prayer" a cappella while standing next to her bed in the darkened room. From what I could ascertain, Charlotte had a deep faith in God. A practicing Episcopalian, Charlotte more or less enjoyed visits by the clergy from the church where I guessed she had attended at one time. We didn't read scripture together but she talked about God fairly often, along with her hope of the existence of heaven. However, I did discover one issue with Charlotte's faith.

Death.

Charlotte told me she was "deathly" afraid of dying. There seemed an unspoken rule to never bring

up the fact with her that all of us have to die some-
day. I truly feel she had convinced herself she was
never going to die. Charlotte told me one night after I
had tucked her in under her covers, "I can't imagine
heaven could be any better than this." She reasoned
because she had no concrete evidence she would go
to heaven; she would just as soon stay alive on earth.
She told me she wasn't going anywhere until she had
confirmation heaven exists and she would be allowed
to enter its gates. I tried to reassure her many times
telling her, "Of course you will be going to heaven,"
but Charlotte remained unconvinced for what would
be a very long, long time.

To help ensure continued good health (and
hopefully avoid death), she visited various physicians
quite frequently. Her date book was often full of
appointments to see the allergist, the eye doctor, the
podiatrist, her personal psychiatrist, or her beloved
primary physician. For two years after I joined her
merry band of nurses, we all worked four-hour shifts,
getting paid for eight. Who could complain? Best of
all, I now had an income to fund spring break trips
which I now planned with great anticipation.

Unfortunately, the easy times proved to be relatively brief. Immediately after suffering a setback
after minor surgery in the spring of 2001, Charlotte's
care became decidedly more challenging. Nursing
aides were added to the payroll enabling her to have
someone with her 24/7 (along with the staff aides and
nurses already employed at her facility). Soon after,

we helped move Charlotte into a one-room "apartment" so she could be physically closer to the nurse's station. Even after her move, we all continued to try to keep her routine as normal as possible. Eventually, she had to take meals in a smaller area at the end of the hallway. Despite her slowly deteriorating physical condition, Charlotte remained resolute about getting the most out of each day. Confined mostly to a wheelchair by now, she could still attend musical events, watch television shows which interested her and of course, find delight in each and every meal (along with afternoon snacks). As she became less mobile, it often took two of us to help move her in and out of wheelchairs and her recliner. There were people coming and going in and out of her small apartment continually and Charlotte thrived on the attention purposefully focused on her. Months gave way to years and it truly appeared Charlotte had figured out a way to live forever.

But of course, age, health, and the passage of time always have the final say. One winter afternoon in 2005, as I came on shift to get "the report" from Charlotte's longtime (and a favorite) nurse Dolores*, I noticed Charlotte's head drooping at an odd angle. I could also see saliva slowly pooling on her lap from her slack mouth. Not wanting to prematurely raise alarms, I reached into my bag and pulled out a pad of paper, writing "Has she been like this all day?" After reading my note, Dolores looked over to Charlotte and turned back to me with a shocked expression while shaking her head emphatically. "No," Dolores whispered, "this is new." Horribly, both of us realized we were witnessing Charlotte having a medical event right before our eyes. The facility staff came quickly to assess the situation, calling 911 soon thereafter.

As we suspected, tests at the hospital where she had been transported to quickly confirmed she had suffered a massive stroke. After being admitted, Charlotte was assigned a spacious private room. This proved particularly helpful because we privately-employed registered nurses were still expected to keep a 24-hour vigil over Charlotte along with her regular hospital nursing staff. I hadn't had any experience working for the super wealthy but surely no one else could receive such attentive care. With the future unknown, Charlotte's nursing aides were put on indefinite leave until further notice.

When I arrived at the hospital for my six-hour shift, I had very little to do. It may sound delightfully easy but the days passed excruciatingly slowly. After arriving at Charlotte's room, I often pulled up a chair next to Charlotte's bed and watched her sleep. The hospital nurses came in to give medications and help me turn Charlotte, but the days seemed interminable. Her situation became increasingly grim over the ensuing weeks. She could not move well, certainly couldn't use the toilet herself or eat regular food. Still, Charlotte stubbornly clinged to life, seemingly continuing her wait for proof of and an invitation to heaven. When and how exactly was this going to happen?

Late winter gave way to spring and finally, as the long summer days approached once more, Charlotte was discharged and allowed to return to her apartment. We privately-employed nurses continued our rotation of long shifts, ensuring someone was with her around the clock. Again, the hours passed so slowly. Charlotte could barely move and slept most of the day. Every two hours we turned her from side to back to side, and when necessary, cleaned and changed her diaper. We loved Charlotte, and despite the hard work, all of us were mindful to provide her prodigious care. The last thing Charlotte needed was bedsores. Her quality of life appeared to be so diminished, but *still*, she seemed to cling to the world of the living.

On a late June day in 2005, while I napped at home, I got a call from Dolores. When I answered, I could tell by her tone of voice something had changed. "Hey, Dolores, what's happened?" I asked, though I was fairly sure of the answer. "I wanted to let you know Charlotte died this afternoon, at 2:18 p.m. I listened quietly trying to fully grasp the full impact of this information as she continued, "I was with her, holding her hand. I told her it was OK to let go. That she was not going to be alone and God was waiting for her in heaven." Tears filled my eyes as I pictured the two of them together with Dolores gently trying to convince Charlotte she did indeed have a heavenly invitation addressed with her name on it. Dolores said that moments after she spoke these particular words, Charlotte finally let go. She died a few months shy of her 90th birthday.

We grieved. Every one of us grieved. With her death, we not only became unemployed but our little community together had come to an abrupt end. With Charlotte as our center, we represented her extended family. In the process, all of us had become like a sisterhood of nurses.

While the shock of her death was still fresh, we were notified that, at Charlotte's request, we were to gather in her apartment the following day to divide up her things among us. She wanted each nurse to have something to remember her by.

The next day, I entered Charlotte's room to find most of the others had already arrived for our "last shift". There were at least thirteen of us crammed into her small room. It was democratically decided to take turns choosing items in the order of how long we'd been employed or known Charlotte.

Because we all cared about each other dearly, the process of division went smoothly. There were no fights over the plastic watering can or the badly tarnished metal towel rack which had obviously seen decades of use. Two nurses verbally tussled a bit over a mohair coat but the afternoon passed quickly with us laughing frequently when remembering funny stories tied to many of the mementos. Through thick and thin, we always tried to find reasons to look for a silver lining. This occasion was particularly special because we knew we were all destined to go our own separate ways after Charlotte's funeral. We knew we'd try to stay in touch but also knew the reality of how difficult this would become as life inevitably would take us on different paths.

We were well into our last item selections when I happened to look up at Charlotte's clock. This plain, ordinary white plastic battery-operated timepiece had been on the wall behind Charlotte's chair for as long as I had known her. I remember willing the hands to move faster on long winter evenings when I still had a long drive home on a lonely stretch of highway after my shift. Because I couldn't leave until my relief came at 11 p.m., I referred to this particular clock as my timeclock. For the six years I worked for Charlotte, this clock had kept perfect time.

And so, hours later on our final afternoon with all of us gathered in Charlotte's room one last time, I looked up at the clock. I immediately noticed something seemed off. The time couldn't be right. It had to be much later than the hands indicated. And then I realized, with a start, the clock hands had stopped. The same clock that for years had reliably indicated when to take Charlotte to dinner, to sing-a-longs, to countless hair appointments, and in particular, to mark the end of hundreds of shifts had quietly but obviously stopped.

But it was the time these hands had stopped which gave me pause, and a peculiar feeling. Still staring at it, I asked rather generally to the ladies in the room, "What time did Charlotte die?"

"2:18," Dolores answered quickly.

And with an amused expression, I announced to everyone, "Well folks, Charlotte seems to be sending us a message. Her clock has stopped at exactly 2:18." The room grew suddenly quiet. It didn't have to be spelled out what an unusual occurrence we'd witnessed.

I believe we all had the same thought as we looked at one another and broke out in big smiles. What an uncanny coincidence! This clock had most certainly been working when we gathered earlier in the day. Most positively, something unusual appeared to be taking place. With cheer in our hearts and smiles on our faces, every one of us raised our hands holding imaginary wine glasses. All together we toasted our beloved benefactor and friend saying aloud, "Hello, Charlotte!" Collectively, we couldn't have been happier believing that Charlotte was letting us know she had received her invitation into heaven. We loved believing she was finally free from all the limitations, physical and mental, she had endured for most of her life.

The clock? I'm not sure which nurse took it home but the whole incident was amusing at the time and I chalked it up to being a notably fun coincidence. After Charlotte's passing, I returned to my full-time "homemaker" role trying to figure out what to do next to keep busy and make a little income. Most of my friends worked outside their home, at least part time. Shortly after Charlotte died, I became increasingly motivated to keep my eyes and ears open for any new work opportunity.

Unfortunately, something not related to work was unfolding during the long hot days of this particular summer. I didn't know it at the time, but the coming months would prove quite difficult to bear. What I couldn't know was that this year in particular marked the beginning of a multitude of heartache, soul searching, faith questioning, and endurance of spirit. Beginning in the spring, my world became forever imprinted with apparent signs happening one after another and another. These "messages", I learned quickly, could not be summoned "on demand". They appeared when they wanted to show themselves, most certainly not as the result of any requests. I have learned both faith and hope are the essential keys to seeing "signs"—along with patience.

And sometimes, they have proved to be a bit amusing.

CHAPTER 2

It's All Greek to Me

Alexa * bounced into my life soon after we moved to Pennsylvania in January 1997. When my family and I moved into our four-bedroom colonial situated on a quiet cul-de-sac, she was the first, and only, person to officially welcome us into the neighborhood. Alexa arrived at our front door with a beautifully wrapped platter of Italian cookies from a local bakery complete with festive ribbons securing the top of the cellophane encased paper plate. I had never seen cookies wrapped so beautifully. Living outside of the South for the first time in my life, her act of hospitality reassured me my family had made a great move despite now living in "Yankee Territory." Home alone with two young children, I felt grateful to be so effusively welcomed to the neighborhood.

Alexa and her husband, Jake*, became instant friends with Pete and me, as if we had known each other for a long, long time.

A year older than me, Alexa was born in 1961 to parents of a strong Greek heritage. Alexa was especially proud of her roots and she worked hard to uphold family traditions passed down from her parents' families. She introduced me to Greek cookies at Christmas and for years, we attended the Greek picnic at her Orthodox church in nearby Media, Pennsylvania. An attractive, brown-eyed, tall brunette extrovert, Alexa always made me feel like we had been friends since childhood. Even better, she and Jake were parents to two children, Danny* and Julie*, close in age to Phil and Henrik. The four children became fast friends, making Friday night suppers together particularly enjoyable. Soon, we were included in their extended family birthday celebrations and picnics. One couldn't ask for better friends.

As the years rolled by, Alexa's children and my boys developed different interests and grew apart but Alexa enthusiastically greeted my sons whenever they encountered each other. On the first day of every school year Alexa would call to them, "Phil, Henrik, come give me a big hug!" when they passed her house while walking to the bus stop. My boys would glance back at me, roll their eyes a bit, before awkwardly approaching Alexa for their yearly "big hug." Having a huge heart, she loved enveloping my sons and telling each of them, "You are a good egg" before they squirmed away as fast as possible. As they grew into their preteen years, Phil, in particular, dreaded the yearly command for a "big hug." Deep down however, I think he appreciated the attention. And, of course, my relationship with Alexa stayed strong. I found it easy to discuss parenting and school-related issues with her, and I looked forward to her parties. You could count on her to host Candlelite Candles, Tupperware, and Pampered Chef home demonstrations to support her friends and their businesses. In fact, when I first moved to Wallingford, I too, sold Pampered Chef. She hosted one of my first, and most successful parties, helping launch my new business. Alexa was "a good egg" herself.

Much to my delight, she also had "an in" with someone at her work who could procure great tickets to home Phillies baseball games. We enjoyed front-row seats behind the visitor's dugout at Veterans Stadium and later, Hall of Fame seats at the newly built Citizens Bank Park. We hooted and howled at these games, which took place in seasons shortly before the Phillies won the World Series in 2008. Always generous, she made the extra effort to get tickets for my Dad and me to attend games when he visited Philadelphia soon after the new park opened.

Those early years flew by as they often do.

Before we knew it, with the millennium's arrival, our elder children were middle school students. Alexa and I didn't see a lot of each other during those years. She loved her full-time job with the Navy as a civil engineer and traveled to Washington, D.C. and Texas for work fairly often. Yet, we managed to keep in touch when we could. Since we first met almost ten years before, she had always appeared to be in good health. I wasn't aware she ever missed a day at work due to illness. So, it was unusual when sometime in the spring of 2004, Alexa started to complain of having a cough and chest discomfort, neither of which improved despite multiple rounds of different antibiotics. At first, doctors said her symptoms were probably related to a bad case of bronchitis. Finally, after weeks of failed medicinal treatments, she called to tell me she was having a bronchoscopy that morning, an exam specifically designed to test and diagnose airway function. I'm not sure either of us expressed being too concerned. After all, we were way too young for anything bad to happen.

I was home when the phone rang sometime mid-afternoon. It was Alexa calling me with a preliminary report. The news wasn't good.

Alexa was ultimately diagnosed with lung cancer. In those days, her specific type of cancer was a fairly quick and certain death sentence. She had treatment options but no cure. It seemed unbelievable. She appeared so vibrant and healthy looking. I remember her being excitedly determined to complete an advanced accreditation in her field in the coming months in spite of her prognosis. For quite a while, Alexa seemed fine. Her treatments took her hair, but not her spirit. It is said one of the best things you can do when you are diagnosed with cancer is to keep a positive outlook. Alexa mastered feeling positive. For many months, her efforts seemed to pay off.

Even though the IV cancer treatment drugs left her often exhausted, she continued to stay upbeat even on days when it was hard for her to get off the couch. Still, as the months continued, her condition slowly deteriorated. On her daughter Julie's thirteenth birthday in late February of 2006, it became apparent she needed more care than she could receive at home. She managed to sing "Happy Birthday" to her daughter, before needing to seek immediate medical attention minutes later. We helped her into her car before Jake drove her to a renowned cancer hospital in Philadelphia. Despite her tremendous will to live, suddenly, her condition appeared dire. We waved goodbye, wondering whether she'd ever return to her home again.

In the following weeks, Alexa went from the hospital to a rehab center before living out her last days in a nursing care facility a mile from our homes. I visited her several times, becoming more astonished how physically she deteriorated between visits. When I last saw her, she wasn't able to speak but she seemed to know me. Her days must have seemed interminable but still, it appeared Alexa wasn't ready to give up. Jake stayed by her side. In fact, during the last months of her illness, he hardly ever left her by herself. Spring turned into the first days of summer as Alexa's condition continued to worsen.

On the morning of June 28, 2006, Jake called me around 5:30. I knew immediately what he was going to tell me when I recognized his voice over the telephone. Indeed, after saying hello to him, he said, "Hey Ellen, I just wanted you to know that Alexa died early this morning," the grief in his voice tangible. Before hanging up, he told me he would be in touch soon about the funeral details. He must have made a million phone calls to friends and relatives. Jake and Alexa had been together since college, been married for two decades, and were devoted parents to two children still too young to fully grasp what had happened within their family. Unbelievably, Alexa was gone, at only 44.

What a loss of a beautiful, smart, talented mother, wife, daughter and dear friend. Her death was probably the first for many young people in our community to experience. I know this was true in the case of my boys, Phil and Henrik. They had never known the feeling of losing a loved one or even someone they personally knew. Alexa's death devastated the entire community. During her illness, many mothers and acquaintances had dropped off meals, religious tokens, and even some sort of flying pig; loaned to Alexa to bring back good health. Her death reminded us all how fragile our time on earth is and to remember each day is not to be taken for granted.

The day of Alexa's funeral arrived. Both sons grumbled a bit about having to wear a sport coat and tie to the service. Just before leaving the house, Pete hurriedly handed me my brand-new cellular phone he had picked up the day before from the AT&T store. This phone, replacing my flip phone, came with a new number. After Pete gave it to me, I took a quick look at it before throwing it in my purse. I didn't know how it worked (nor did I care at the moment) or even look to see if Pete had turned the thing on. In those days, I considered a cell phone more or less a safety device, to use in case of a car breakdown. I had other priorities at the moment, such as getting to the funeral service on time. "Hurry guys, we've got to go!", I yelled at my three men, hoping they had managed to get their ties on relatively straight.

When we arrived at the church, we found the parking lot as full as a stadium during playoff season. Seeing few places left to park, we had no option but to drive onto the grass field adjacent to the church. It appeared the entire town of Wallingford had come to pay respects.

When the four of us entered the cavernous sanctuary, you could hear a pin drop. We first saw a long line leading up to Alexa's casket where she was laid out. Jake and his children stood close by, receiving the hundreds of mourners. When I walked up to look into the casket, she took my breath away. Alexa looked like Sleeping Beauty, her long brown hair falling across her shoulders with her countenance reflecting one of being at true peace. I found it hard to believe she would never wake again.

An almost tangible sadness engulfed the entire room like a tidal wave. After going through the viewing line, my men and I found seats near the back. As I sat down, I noted my boys' elementary school principal seated on the pew directly in front of us. For some reason, she was in fact the only other person I noticed. The whole scene seemed surreal and totally dreamlike. "Surely this isn't happening," I thought as I looked forward. "Alexa was too young to die."

Her service was lovely. What gave me particular solace at the time was thinking Alexa was no longer incapacitated or in pain. The priest delivering her eulogy stood as a commanding figure in his brilliant white robes and beautiful head piece called a kamilavka. The message and music felt comforting. Still, my mind drifted as the service came to a conclusion with the priest giving information about the luncheon Jake and his family had invited all mourners to attend immediately following the service.

Just then I heard the irritating ring of a phone. "Brr-ring"—"Brrrrrrinnnng"— BRIIIINNNGGGG!"

"What the heck?", I thought, jolted out of my reverie.

This was not a ring "tone," but an impossibly shrill jangle, seemingly bouncing off the walls of the octagonal walled church with a ceiling soaring to the heavens. The subsequent ringing seemed to bounce off every wall angle ensuring every mourner in the room could hear it. At first, I looked around disapprovingly for the idiot who had left their phone turned on during Alexa's service. I couldn't wait to discover the rude culprit. And as I turned, listening right, then left, then right again, a horrible realization slowly but earnestly dawned on me.

The ringing echoing close to my ears was coming from my own little black bag on the floor!!! And with each unanswered ring, the horrible noise grew louder and louder so by the sixth ring, I knew everyone in the church had become aware that I, Ellen Oetinger, was the one who had left my phone on.

Worse yet, after fumbling around for the phone itself, I realized in horror, I didn't even know how to turn the ringer off. I had never seen this phone before in my life! During those chaotic moments, I felt all eyes were on me. I even distinctly remember noticing my son's principal turn her head and give me "the look" elementary school principals must certainly master to keep unruly children in line. Her giving me "the look" wasn't meant to be unkind I'm sure, but nevertheless, it added to my intense feelings of embarrassment and humiliation.

Finally—after hitting enough buttons, the horrendous noise stopped. It didn't matter though because by this time, the service had ended. With a reddened face, I quickly grabbed my bag and headed for the exit, phone in hand.

I didn't look right or left while flying furiously out of the church as quickly as possible.

Once out of earshot, I quickly marched up to my elder son. "Phil, who did you give this number to?

Who was trying to call me?" Phil seemed to be the logical one to blame since he loved electronics and their buttons and didn't have a phone of his own. Deep down, I knew he had nothing to do with the phone call during the service but it still seemed to make sense to ask the "usual suspects"–my children.

Phil turned to me, declaring adamantly, "It wasn't me Mom! How could I have given the number to anyone? I don't even know it."

His calm and matter of fact statement stopped me in my tracks. Because he was right. No one could have purposefully tried to call any of us on this unfamiliar phone. None of us knew the number yet, especially me. Pete had written it down and taped it to the back of the phone but I certainly hadn't had the opportunity to memorize or share the number with anyone.

Practically in tears, I fled to the car. I felt mortified that I had caused such a disturbance during Alexa's beautiful service. I wanted to hide from everyone.

Later in the day, Pete told me, "I think I have a way to find out who made the phone call."

"Really Pete? Oh my gosh, that would be awesome!" I couldn't wait to find out who tried to call, possibly finding some redemption. Cell phones were still relatively new to me but so far, I found them to be terribly intrusive.

Turning on my phone, he quickly punched in the number to call it back—waiting for someone to answer.

Within a short time, Pete took the phone from his ear and said, "That's odd." Noticing the puzzled look on his face, I said, "What's odd? What happened?"

Looking up at me rather perplexed, he calmly replied, "The area code is one in Texas. I got an automated message informing me, "The number you have dialed is disconnected, *not* currently in use."

My mouth dropped open. "But how can this be?" We both looked at each other in bewilderment. This made absolutely no sense.

And then—moments later, it dawned on me there could only be one logical explanation to this whole mystery; if one can believe in the ability of communicating from another world.

Please bear in mind Alexa was a fun-loving extrovert who seemed to find the silver lining, particularly when things weren't going exactly as planned. Over the years of our friendship, we found it easy to burst out laughing over funny jokes and situations.

Simply put, I firmly believe, even to this day, my mysterious phone call had been from Alexa, "ringing" in to let me know "spiritually" she had attended and enjoyed her service. She certainly had to be pleased by the number in attendance. "Yes," I easily convinced myself. Alexa most certainly had to be behind the mysterious phone call. With everyone so, so sad, it would have been like her to reassure those she loved she was in a good place and at peace after a long, hard-fought battle against her cancer.

I ruminated a bit about what had happened before walking over to check in on Jake. I especially wanted to apologize in person for the rude phone interruption during his wife's service. Upon hearing my humble apology, he told me, "I vaguely remember hearing a phone but I didn't give it much thought." His kind response immediately put me more at ease.

Taking in a deep breath, I went on to explain about the disconnected "party" which had apparently tried to contact me during his wife's service. Deciding to go out on a limb, I added, "I know you might think this is nuts, but I truly think the phone "call" was somehow Alexa. I think she wants us to know she is fine and apparently a bit of heaven is in Texas."

Jake gently laughed when I told him this, calming my nerves even more. I still felt horrible over the whole situation but for a quick moment, we both smiled. It was nice to see him chuckle a bit.

Later in the evening, as Pete and I reviewed the whole incident again, I remembered what had happened in Charlotte's room the previous year (almost to the day). At the time, both incidents were chalked up to being uncanny coincidences. And then—we forgot about them. Until another strange, yet true, event happened in the coming months.

CHAPTER 3

An Angel with a Badge

"Show kindness and hospitality to strangers, for
you may be entertaining an angel unawares."
—Hebrews 3:2

Summer, 2007. Alexa had been gone now over
a year. A lot had happened since her funeral,
especially with my elder son, Phil. If aviators can be
born naturals, then Phil seemed to exactly fit the bill.
Before he even had his driver's license, Phil soloed in
a Cessna 152, a small but sturdy two-seater airplane.
How he found himself as a budding pilot seemed
to be a part of God's grand plan for him—if one
believes in such things.

Always quiet and serious minded, Phil enjoyed
his passion for anything aviation related even as a

small boy. If he found a sheet of cardboard, he'd build an airport runway system complete with planes and baggage carts. At age eight, he discovered the world of flight simulators on the house computer. He trained on lots of "simulated" planes with earnest intent. He always insisted on being the Pilot in Command (PIC) which is most definitely a great quality for any promising pilot. As Phil grew into a young adult, his love for anything flight related never faded. In fact, his interest became more than a passing hobby by the time he turned 13. A quiet teenager, he often gamed at home in his room on his self-built computer. Increasingly enamored of anything aviation related, he started mastering the art of flying remote control (RC) planes at 14. To buy bigger and better airplanes, Phil created his own business of converting VHS tapes to DVDs for my friends and worked weekends at a nearby sandwich shop. Weeks before Phil's fourteenth birthday, Pete and I sent Phil by commercial plane to visit my parents in Kentucky. My father had made arrangements for him to attend a flight camp in nearby Lexington. Unwittingly, my father changed the course of Phil's life by the end of the first day at aviation camp.

Late that first day of camp, my Dad's phone number popped up on my phone.

Answering with a bit of anxiety, I was surprised to hear it was actually Phil calling. Before I could ask any questions about his day, he loudly announced,

"MOM! I know what I want to do for the rest of my life!"

"What's that, Phil?", I said, relieved to hear him so upbeat.

"I want to fly!"

I wanted to cry. I had never heard Phil so happy.

With the die cast, by the ripe old age of 14, Phil had plotted his entire future in the world of aviation. Now it would seem, all he had to do was plan how to incorporate his passion for flying into his future education.

For a while, flying RC planes seemed enough for Phil. Then destiny intervened.

In late July 2006, on a hot weekend afternoon, the four of us decided to embark on a family outing. Phil suggested we tour a nearby helicopter museum in West Chester, PA, less than an hour from our home. After parking, we ventured into the museum building with Phil eagerly in the lead. The four of us wandered about, enjoying the exhibits, especially the antique and experimental helicopters on display. Outside the museum building, you can still see an old Osprey—a military aircraft that can take off and land like a helicopter and fly like a plane—with its massive rotors tilted up, frozen in time. We explored the inside of the copter marveling at its size and the engineering behind its design. After my men and I finished our examination of the Osprey's cavernous fuselage, we found ourselves standing on the blistering hot pavement wondering what to do next. Phil looked over and pointed out what appeared to be a small airport. Various sizes and makes of small planes were parked outside of the modest low-lying brick building.

Out of the blue Phil asked, "Can I take flying lessons?" Now I'm sure most parents might quickly say, "What? No way. You're not going up in one of those tiny planes." But we knew this request was inevitable. And I personally had no interest in repeating my mother's mistake. I remember being quite interested myself in learning how to fly. As a young girl, airplanes captivated me. I still kind of resent that when I announced to my mother, "I'm going to be a pilot when I grow up!", she responded rather unkindly, "No, you can't be a pilot. You won't be strong enough." Being only nine or ten at the time, I mistakenly believed her.

With Phil now days away from driving an automobile (and certainly being plenty strong), we decided then and there to motor over to the airport to explore more. We noticed the little "Learn to Fly Here" sign as we made the right turn to our destination, the Brandywine Airport. Walking into the small office of the school we encountered a chatty, middle-aged man sitting at the desk who introduced himself as Fred*. He enthusiastically offered us literature regarding the different planes in his fleet, along with insurance details, fuel pricing, and a run down on the costs of lessons. Fred gave us further details on his school's maintenance and safety records before we told him we'd go home to think on it. Overall, we left feeling this "school" could be a great place for Phil to try out his "wings" so to speak.

Pete and I talked it over the same evening, ultimately deciding flight lessons could be something positive for Phil to do in his high school years. Loving a bargain, we appreciated that the school offered a "first flight free" promotion before any monetary commitments had to be made.

Possibly being a "helicopter" (no pun intended) mom, I called the school to make arrangements for Phil to take his first lesson. Talking to Fred again, I explained that my son, being a quiet, relatively shy guy, needed an exceptionally mild-mannered instructor who wouldn't bark instructions at students. Fred said he understood and thought he had the "perfect instructor" for Phil. On July 19th, 2006, I drove my eldest son back to the Brandywine Airport to meet the man who would hopefully teach Phil how to fly—safely. First though, Phil needed to like and trust this man.

We walked into the tiny office and met Hagan*, an instantly likeable young man who looked no more than a kid of twenty-five (which turned out to be his actual age). After we all made our introductions, I followed them up the stairs where Hagan told me I could wait during Phil's lesson. I'm not too sure who felt more excited, Phil or me. Quickly becoming my favorite opportunity to live vicariously through one of my sons, this adventure already proved exciting!

Looking out the window, I watched as Hagan showed Phil how to perform the prep work on the Cessna 152 by checking the tires, wing condition and fuel levels. After they climbed in, it wasn't long before the propeller spun to life and they began to taxi away. I immediately liked Hagan and, though he wasn't a veteran flight instructor, I felt Phil was in good hands. I watched as the small white plane, with the call sign of 6497M, motored toward the end of the runway before disappearing from view. A few minutes later, I held my breath as the little plane raced down the runway gently lifting into the air with apparent ease. As this was Phil's first flight in this particular plane, I assumed Hagan must be at the controls. The thought reduced my nervousness.

Approximately 30 minutes later, the pilot (again, I assumed it had to be Hagan) landed the plane easily before guiding it back to the parking area. Shy Phil had the cutest grin on his face. When he saw me, he said it went "great" and immediately requested to continue with lessons. Hagan gave Phil his first official logbook and while recording the first entry, he commented out loud that Phil "certainly knew what he was doing." It turns out Phil had piloted his first flight with Hagan almost 100 percent of the time. With pride and relief that Phil had found a great after school activity, I signed him up for additional lessons by putting a big deposit into his flight school account. Phil hadn't quite turned 16 and didn't have his driver's permit, but he was flying airplanes! I had never known him to be so happy.

Hagan and Phil spent hours over the coming months practicing, with Phil rapidly moving toward his first solo flight. On January 11, 2007, a few months after Phil's first lesson with Hagan, the confident-looking instructor got out of the Cessna after a very short flight and began walking back toward the airport building. "Oh, my Lord," I said to myself as my stomach did a backflip. "This is it!" Sure enough, Hagan picked up the walkie talkie from the office desk before heading out to the tarmac in front of the building. Everyone there knew what this meant. Phil was about to take his first solo flight!

I'm not sure who felt more nervous; Phil, Hagan or me. Hagan allowed me to walk out to the deck to stand with him. For his first time flying solo, Phil took off flawlessly, rising "up," "up," "up," before disappearing into the westward sky in the tiny plane. Remembering the moment clearly still makes my heart pound years later. Hagan and I stood there silently, waiting, and waiting for his return. Time literally seemed to stand still, both of us straining to hear the wonderful sound of an engine announcing an impending landing.

And then, suddenly, we saw the beautiful little plane, coming in for its final approach with my son, "Captain Phil" at the controls, all by himself! Hagan had the walkie talkie in case Phil needed to talk to him for guidance (or help). Fortunately, the only words we heard were Phil declaring over the microphone "Brandywine traffic, November 6497 Mike runway 27 short final".

Phil landed the plane perfectly. Tears filled my eyes with so much pride and happiness for my son. I loved seeing him find success doing something he obviously enjoyed. Phil parked and tied down the plane. Walking back into the lounge wearing a big grin, he exclaimed, "That was awesome!"

With the solo flight behind him, Phil and Hagan worked on all the maneuvers pilots must master before getting certified as a private pilot. The staff had become our extended family as the summer of 2007 arrived. On many summer afternoons, a group of us would gather for picnics or cookouts after Phil's lessons. Even the airport managers, John and Jay, often joined us for burgers on the grill. Increasingly eager to fly commercially, Hagan was applying for jobs with passenger airlines. Phil raced to achieve his private pilot certificate before Hagan left for bigger planes.

I give this background information because as the months progressed, Hagan became not only Phil's instructor but also his mentor and friend. Besides entrusting my son's safety to the young instructor, I personally give Hagan credit for helping Phil become more confident and positive about his future, most certainly headed for a career in aviation.

Our family trip that summer to Cape Cod was bittersweet. Though Phil managed to go on a couple of outings with us, it was clear he would rather be at the airport either working or continuing with his flight lessons. I couldn't help but feel that real changes were coming soon.

I was right.

They started with a phone call from Hagan. Phoning us two days before the end of our trip he had both good and bad news.

Starting with his good news first, he happily shared he had gotten a job offer with a regional airline finally allowing him to fulfil his dream of flying passenger planes.

His bad news: his good friend Steve* had been killed days before in a motor vehicle accident. Hagan didn't give us any details of how it happened but his joy of being hired to fly passenger planes appeared heavily subdued by his friend's untimely death.

Weeks later, Hagan talked to me a bit about the accident. On the evening of the crash, Steve had asked Hagan to meet and hang out at a nearby popular bar. Hagan told Steve he couldn't get together as he was busy preparing for the upcoming final testing with an interviewing airline. Apparently, Steve went out anyway; later being instantly killed when the car he was driving apparently slammed into the back of a semi-truck. Because no one knew the details of what Steve had been doing prior to the crash, one could think that perhaps alcohol or another substance played into the reason for the fatal accident. All Hagan knew for sure was his friend had died on the night he had been asked to meet up with him, and he felt horrible.

Fast forward to the spring of 2009. Phil, now an aviation student at the University of North Dakota, found himself working hard flying a larger Cessna in much rougher conditions. Fifteen-year-old Henrik was at home busy trying to figure out his own interests and potential college choices.

With the men in my house needing me less and less, I decided to concentrate on my own career, and began working three days a week with a group of interventional radiologists.

Three of the docs were getting more and more busy developing and growing their independent vein center at a nearby medical clinic. Thanks to newer technology, the business of treating varicose veins was starting to boom! I found being a part of this new enterprise terribly exciting because my main nursing assignment utilized a particularly strong skill of mine: using conversation to help keep patients comfortable during their treatments. The procedures are safe for the majority of patients. Most days, the cases were very much routine, until one extraordinary morning.

I walked out to the main lobby area of the large imaging practice calling out the name for the next patient.

"John*?" I asked out to the group of people waiting in the large room.

"I'm John," said a nice looking, though a bit nervous appearing, middle-aged man sitting next to a woman who I assumed had come along to drive him home after the procedure.

After he told me his birthday to establish that I had the correct "John," he rose from his chair and walked toward me.

I asked John to change into a gown and fuzzy brown socks. John's preliminary testing had already indicated the large vein running down the whole of his right leg was diseased. Despite trying to appear tough, John certainly looked a tad nervous. Nervous people usually like to talk. Hopefully helping John find the whole experience less frightening, I distracted him with lively chit chat while the doc worked on his leg.

I launched into the usual basic questions such as, "Where do you live?" "What do you do for a living?" and "Do you have family in the area?" As expected, John began eagerly telling me about his family before sharing the details of his career.

"I'm a police officer," he told me soon after Dr. Baker* began injecting numbing lidocaine along the length of the vein.

"Wow, that's pretty cool. Where do you usually patrol?"

As he described the perimeters of his usual beat, I smiled, knowing this area well. I had traveled along these roads often when taking Phil to the airport for his lessons. I found it fascinating to hear where he and his police buddies often sat in their cars watching for speeders. During our conversation, I made a mental note to stay close to the speed limit when traveling these particular roads, as they were apparently heavily monitored.

While he rattled off the names of some of the roads he regularly patrolled, I remembered the horrible car accident that had happened a couple of years prior involving Hagan's friend. The accident had occurred in the approximate area where John said he patrolled.

With some trepidation, I asked John, "Do you by chance remember a fatal crash that happened in the summer of 2007 involving a driver slamming into the back of a truck?" I gave the road name but told him I didn't know exactly where the accident had occurred.

Without pause, John said, "I know exactly the accident you are talking about. I was the first responder to arrive at the crash site. I witnessed the retrieval of the body from the wreckage. Terrible accident."

In total shock, I couldn't help but wonder about the odds of talking to someone who had been with Hagan's friend soon after the deadly crash. I explained to John how Hagan felt awful for not meeting up with his friend; forever wondering if he somehow could have prevented the fatal crash.

John told me, "I'll look into the details of the accident and let you know if I find out anything when I come back for my next appointment. I don't remember what the final report said."

"Thank you," I responded, still astounded at the whole "coincidence." After work the same afternoon, I immediately called Hagan and without giving away personal details about my patient, explained how I had come to meet the officer who was first on the scene of his friend's accident. He too was amazed and curious.

A week later, John returned for his follow-up visit.

No sooner had John settled back onto the examination table, when he shared with me the results of the report. "There were no alcohol or drugs in the victim's system", John informed me. "His death was ruled "an accident." Period.

"Wow," I remember thinking to myself. The report still didn't explain what had exactly happened, but I was somehow comforted that the fatal accident didn't appear to be the result of impaired driving. I thanked John for looking into the matter, feeling grateful for the unusual coincidence of our crossing paths. The treatment in John's leg had been successful and the bulging varicose veins in his lower leg were already vastly reduced one week later. I overheard talk between John and Dr. Baker about treating the varicose veins in John's left leg, also showing signs of disease.

Strangely enough; however, I never saw John again. As far as I know, he never came back for any further follow up visits after that appointment. He had seemed to vanish. Again, I couldn't help but feel how coincidental it was we should meet.

I quickly got back in touch with Hagan, passing on the information given to me. Hagan thanked me, expressed relief at knowing the toxicology report was negative, and stated he too found it unbelievable the police officer's and my paths should cross.

I'll never forget my patient, the police officer, or perhaps more accurately, an angel with a badge? After now experiencing these three signs fairly close together, I began to believe something more was happening. When my husband encountered the next sign, we both knew we were in the midst of a series of profoundly real phenomena.

CHAPTER 4

Deadly Deviant "Genes"

B y now, I had experienced three recent interesting "coincidences" making me more and more curious. When telling a few friends the stories of Alexa, Charlotte, and my angel cop, everyone listened politely agreeing my short collection of tales perhaps belonged on an episode of "The Twilight Zone." Still, none of us gave any of them much serious thought. More unsettling developments were going on at the time.

Shortly before Charlotte's death, my best friend's mother, Doris, returned a bit early from her yearly snowbird vacation in Florida. She had suddenly developed ominous physical symptoms in her abdomen in the previous weeks. When my friend, Kristin, called informing me her mother was returning home to Boston early for some initial testing, we both hoped nothing was seriously wrong. An amazing, vivacious woman in her early 60s, Doris possessed incredible energy and an indomitable spirit. She represented Kristin's family as a true matriarch in every sense of the word and was deeply loved by Kristin and her two older brothers.

Wasting no time, Doris underwent initial testing. Unfortunately, the news wasn't good.

Doris' tests showed she had advanced ovarian cancer; surgery recommended immediately.

It was Doris' good fortune she lived outside of Boston, not too far from world-renowned Brigham and Women's Hospital, noted for its excellent reputation for cancer treatment. Doris recovered well after surgery in June 2005 and immediately rallied the troops for the fight of her life, or more accurately, the fight *for* her life. Biopsies showed her cancer had spread to her bowel, foreboding news. Nevertheless, optimist Doris couldn't mope around long feeling sorry for herself. A woman of action, she immediately began chemo treatments with earnest tenacity. For a long while, the doctors were hopeful her surgery and post op cancer treatments would ultimately cure her.

Kristin drove up to New England often to check on her mother and accompany her to the many doctors' appointments her care required. Months passed, then years. When my family and I vacationed on Cape Cod the summer of 2007, we stayed in a cottage across the street from where Doris and her husband Harvey lived year-round. Ever the gracious hostess, she invited me and my men over for a small cocktail party. In spite of her appearing a bit tired, we had a delightful evening. By summer end, we all became more and more hopeful she had indeed "caught the cancer in time".

I wanted more than anything for Doris to beat her disease. My dear friend revered her mother and theirs was the kind of relationship a mother and daughter can only dream of. Doris and Harvey also had a one in-a-million marriage. Both depended on each other for everything and when you were with them, you could feel the strong kinetic energy they exuded together. Doris had a tremendous drive to live, fueled by her family who needed her so much. Two years rolled by with the treatments appearing to extend Doris' well-being. She always found a reason to laugh and her intense positivity helped us all feel more confident she was going to beat her disease.

During Christmas 2007, we four shared the holidays with Kristin and her family including Doris, Harvey, and Kristin's gregarious brother Barney. A truly joyous time, we celebrated the yuletide dinner together with cautious optimism. This was surely going to be one more of many Christmases to come. Pete took videos of the whole evening with our antique Quasar VHS camera to record a multitude of family stories, copious amounts of laughter and evidence of a great deal of love. With optimism in our hearts but knowing the reality, we made a point to enjoy every minute together. At least this one special Christmas would live forever on film.

2008 came and went as Doris continued to hold her own. To keep their thoughts off the negatives of the disease, Doris and Kristin put their creative minds together and developed a unique product specifically designed to help other cancer patients. It is a wrap with special openings for medication delivery. By the spring of 2009, the new product was introduced to the public with a big party at Kristin's home. Doris was determined as ever to attend.

She remained present for most of the fun event. While she still looked beautiful, I remember feeling concerned she seemed more tired than usual. Nevertheless, it was gratifying to see Doris and Kristin enjoy well-deserved time in the limelight. A local news crew showed up to film a segment featuring their wrap which was touted as "One of the great new products of 2009".

The months continued to pass but unfortunately, Doris' prognosis became less hopeful. Doris tried experimental treatments but, her cancer proved relentless. I found it heart wrenching watching Kristin slowly accept the dismaying fact her mom would most certainly not have much longer to live. Although, I think it would be an error to use the word "accept." Despite her mother's physical deterioration and increasing pain, I don't remember Kristin acknowledging her mother could die.

Spring of 2010 brought out the azaleas and the green of the trees again but with the lengthening daylight came the certain reality Kristin could not help her mother any longer from a distance. By mid-May, Doris' condition warranted round the clock care with Doris insisting only Kristin could provide the help she needed. In addition, Doris reluctantly accepted hospice care, though she remained adamant her daughter be with her on a daily basis. I couldn't do much but support my good friend by listening when she called occasionally.

I shared my previous experiences of the apparent signs "received" from Charlotte and Alexa with Kristin before she left Wallingford for her final visit with her mother. Kristin didn't laugh or say to me, "You're crazy." Instead, she found the stories interesting and even a bit believable. During one conversation between us, Kristin said she had shared my stories of signs with her mom. They discussed the possibility of Doris sending a sign of hope and remembrance, validating how much they loved each other and always would, right into eternity. After some thought, Doris told Kristin she would come back to visit from the afterlife as a lively and quick hummingbird. The notion seemed to give Kristin some solace.

As the days progressed, Kristin took over complete care for her mom, including giving her mother more and more pain medication to help relieve Doris' excruciating discomfort.

Kristin found herself in an impossible situation. Until the day she died, Doris remained totally "ticked off" that her cancer certainly appeared to be winning. Kristin gave her mother the best care anyone could receive but ultimately Doris lost her battle.

Doris passed on June 29, 2010, leaving behind a devoted husband, three wonderful grandchildren, two sons and her amazing daughter, Kristin.

Kristin returned home shortly after her mom's death engulfed in unremitting grief. She had lost her mother and her best friend. Personally, I didn't know what best to do: try to be more present or give her and her family more space. For the time being, I chose to give them space. I told Pete about Doris choosing to visit as a hummingbird after she died. Neither of us gave this any additional thought. After all, hummingbird sightings had been rare for us. In fact, at the time, we couldn't remember ever seeing a hummingbird on our property.

Weeks passed. The summer "daze" continued with Wallingford experiencing its usual brutal heat and humidity. On one such mid-afternoon, Pete decided it would be a good idea to go up on a ladder to the second story of our house and clean the gutters.

"You're nuts," I told him, as I meandered over to my next-door neighbor Dee's house not wanting to be any part of Pete's apparent madness. Finding her home, we made ourselves comfortable at her large outdoor table with our glasses of wine before catching up.

It wasn't long though before we were interrupted by my husband. Pete came zipping over to Dee's back yard calling out my name. Obviously, he hadn't fallen and broken anything, but I could tell by the urgency in his voice something was distressing him. "Ellen? Ellen!" he called out as he approached the deck stairs.

In his usual clipped manner of speaking when he's pumped up, he exclaimed while pointing back at the house, "You should give Kristin a call and check on her right now!"

Clearly puzzled at his unusual statement, I asked him, "Why? Are you ok?"

Pete said quite deliberately while pointing up toward the gutter, "Because Doris just came to visit me and I'm thinking she is worried about Kristin."

"What?"

Pete went on to explain he saw a gorgeous, almost effervescent green hued hummingbird appear out of nowhere while he was cleaning the gunk from the gutter 15 feet off the ground. The tiny bird hovered remarkably close to his face making it impossible for him to not notice it. Knowing about the sign between Doris and Kristin, this sighting caught his attention immediately. Pete reasoned it had to be Doris. Why else would a hummingbird come from nowhere to seek out a human on a second-story ladder unless it had something "to say?"

Dashing back to the house, I yelled back a quick goodbye to Dee. When Kristin answered her phone, without giving any details, I said, "Hey, it's me Ellen. I think it's important you come over as soon as possible."

Within minutes, she rang my front doorbell.

My dear friend and I sat on my living room sofa for a long while. She talked and cried, and then talked and cried more while describing in detail those final weeks she achingly endured with her mother. She expressed her terrible grief and guilt over feeling she could have done more. Most of all; however, she shared her emotions about her all-consuming feeling of loss. Though her mother's passing had occurred more than a month hence, her grief remained more than she could seemingly bear.

After Kristin shared for a long while, somewhat cautiously, I told her about Pete's hummingbird sighting. Kristin listened. She didn't laugh it off. I don't remember her saying anything other than she believed her mother was trying to let her know she was "OK" but was worried about her. She and I were able to find a level of comfort with this thought and she left thanking me for the opportunity to vent her emotions so freely.

Kristin continued to grieve for months after her mother died. On a positive note, she has told me on more than one occasion that when she spots a hummingbird, she finds comfort, remembering her mother with a smile instead of tears. Doris died the certain physical death we all face, but her loving spirit appears to have taken flight and will be with her loving daughter always.

Years later, after Kristin read this story, she added details she had not shared with me before.

Kristin and Harvey feel deeply that Doris visited them soon after Doris' physical death. The first encounter occurred June 30th, the day after her mother died. In deep mourning, she was at her parents' house with Harvey and Kristin's brother Barney. "We were gathered in the kitchen at Mom's house and it was cocktail hour. All of a sudden, a hummingbird came to visit at the window right outside where we were all sitting. The tiny bird opened its wings as if to greet us with a big hello." My own eyes widened as she went on to say, "The hummingbird came back three evenings in a row. By the third night, we were eagerly awaiting its return. When it appeared at the window again, we exclaimed, "Hey Mom!"

"But," Kristin continued, "After the third night, we never saw the hummingbird again. Harvey bought nectar, feeders, even planted bushes in the following years to attract hummingbirds but none have come back." Kristin told me Harvey still hopes for another appearance of "Doris" but he hasn't seen a hummingbird again. Clearly, her mom is now in the most wonderful place. In my opinion, she wanted everyone to know she was with them during their most intense period of grief before living again in pain -free peace in life eternal.

The hummingbird's visit, sign or coincidence? By now, neither Pete, Kristin, nor I needed any further convincing that messages from the afterlife are possible. Receiving these signs had given us comforting feelings of solace, which turned out to be a good thing.

Something unusually spooky was going on.

After the hummingbird, I told Pete these weren't coincidences. Any leftover doubts he harbored were quickly erased after we both witnessed the next sign—together.

CHAPTER 5

Off to the Races!

Growing up, our family time revolved around cocktail hour. At exactly 5:30 p.m., those of us at home gathered in our living room to replay the day's events. My dad must have loved gin and tonics because I distinctly remember crunching on the ice cubes after he finished his drink (interestingly, I can't stand the beverage today). Cocktail hour is also remembered as a special time at my larger extended family gatherings such as Thanksgiving and Christmas. As one of the younger grandchildren, I was often "discouraged" from hanging with my older siblings and cousins. "Little Ellen" took refuge on a three-legged brass stool by the fireplace at my grandmother's house where I quietly sat and listened to what my aunts and uncles and grandmother had to say before gathering around the table for dinner.

While balancing on the odd little stool, I learned about state and world politics, town gossip, and happenings with the family at large. I only saw one uncle, my dad's elder brother Bob, at our family holiday meals. His quiet but magnetic personality always made me look at him in awe literally and figuratively. Frankly, as I entered my teen years, he intimidated me so much I scarcely said a word to him. If he did happen to ask me a question, he expected my response to be succinct, no more than five or six words. He had no time for small talk. Trust me, this kind of communication with someone keeps a person on their toes. Though encounters with him sometimes scared me to death, he turned out to positively influence my life in ways I couldn't even imagine possible as a girl. While I never knew my Uncle Bob well, from what I do know, he lived a remarkable life.

He had been a successful litigator in Louisville in a long-established law firm and served as Attorney General for the state of Kentucky from 1964 to 1968. Active his whole life, he always dressed dapper and never, ever talked about age. I can remember as a young girl wanting to wish him a happy 60th birthday only to be firmly told by my grandmother Mimi, "Do *not* mention his birthday!" Being terrified of being reprimanded again, I never again uttered a "Happy Birthday" to Uncle Bob. As he aged into his 80s, I figured his strict abhorrence of acknowledging birthdays did indeed help increase his life expectancy; though I'm fairly convinced his longevity didn't go quite as planned.

Uncle Bob certainly appeared to love retirement. He golfed, traveled, and enjoyed going to the racetrack—often. On a lark, he once took me to a nearby "boat" which is actually a permanent faux riverboat moored on the banks of the Ohio River in southern Indiana to facilitate this particular type of legal gambling. There he taught me the intricacies of shooting craps. And on that particular day, I was on fire! I came away from the table with not only the hundred dollars he advanced to me, but with a few bucks more. We had a great time; however, after we returned home, I knew the addictive gambling bug wasn't going to bite me. I had lived too poorly as a younger woman to ever find it "fun" to bet potential food and travel money away.

My Uncle Bob remained mystical to me during the entire time I knew him. I saw him as a tall, imposing man who was well liked at the private club where his friends called him "the General." After Pete and I became engaged, Uncle Bob sponsored us so we could have our reception at his beautiful country club when we married in 1987. Years later, he proposed us for membership at the same club where after joining, Pete and I spent many a day improving our tennis game. I revered and respected my Uncle Bob though I never knew him well and, from what I was told by my father, apparently few did.

As he aged into his late 70s, Uncle Bob suffered two strokes years apart. He recovered well after his first one following knee surgery. It was during this time that he and I got better acquainted and we enjoyed our casino adventure and an occasional beverage together. This was also the same period of time that my sister's health began taking a rapid turn for the worse.

My relationship with my sister Lisa was the main impetus for my visits to Kentucky during this time. While I loved my uncle, it was my sister's health situation that took me back and forth to Kentucky so often. She was almost 50 years old in 2004 when she received the definitive diagnosis of Multiple Sclerosis (MS). Once a gifted athlete, she found that the disease quickly whittled away her strength and mobility. Worse, the plaque-like lesions MS causes settled along her spinal column, causing her excruciating spasmodic pain made worse with eating or sitting upright. As Lisa celebrated her big five-O, she could no longer care for herself alone. With great fortitude, she moved back home with our parents, settling into one of the three small bedrooms in their ranch home in Shelbyville, Kentucky.

One advantage of her moving back home with my parents was Uncle Bob frequently visited to check on his niece. Uncle Bob and Lisa particularly enjoyed discussing state politics and all sports-related topics. Though still an enigma personally to both of us, he was extremely generous with his time spent with my sister as she became more and more an invalid.

My sister's living situation changed just before Uncle Bob suffered his second stroke. She could no longer live in Shelbyville with my parents because of her worsening handicap. At the same time, my uncle had to move into a nearby nursing home because of his limited mobility. As the months progressed after his second stroke, I can only imagine how long my uncle's days must have felt. According to my father, as fall of 2010 approached, my usually upbeat Uncle Bob became more and more despondent, no longer allowing visitors, even his youngest brother, my dad.

By the last week of October, Uncle Bob's situation became grave. Dad called me, saying, "It's not looking good for brother Bob. It won't be long." I could hear loving resignation in his voice.

Uncle Bob finally "slipped away" (a common family euphemism) on October 30, 2010. I don't want to sound trite, but his death seemed to me to truly be "a blessing." The "General" was finally free from the physical limitations his strokes imposed. If ever someone deserved to find peace, I felt strongly my Uncle Bob did.

I wanted to attend his funeral the following weekend. Unfortunately, because he died close to the time of the famed Breeders' Cup horse racing festivities taking place in Louisville, procuring a seat on a plane going anywhere near Louisville or Lexington, Kentucky, was impossible. I wanted very much to go and pay my respects to a man who had been so influential in my life. After making a failed last-ditch effort, with Hagan's help, to secure a pass to any airport within a 200-mile radius from Louisville, I had to resign myself to the impossibility of attending. Uncle Bob's passing had been the first family death in over 25 years. I felt so frustrated that I couldn't get back "home" to properly pay my respects and be with my grieving father.

Uncle Bob's private burial was held in early November 2010 at Grove Hill Cemetery, where many generations of my family have been laid to rest. My parents were among those gathered around the graveside after a much larger visitation held earlier in the week. Although Uncle Bob was five years older than my father, Dad always looked up to his elder brother with deep affection. While my father had few close friends, he and Uncle Bob had a familial bond which became stronger as they aged. In fact, my dad was one of the few people Uncle Bob allowed to visit in his last months of life.

During Uncle Bob's funeral preparations, visitation, and service, the Breeders' Cup festivities were well under way at Churchill Downs in Louisville. Had Uncle Bob been alive and well, he'd have most certainly been there, in his usual box, with the Daily Racing Form in hand.

Meanwhile, back in Wallingford, on Friday night November 5th, Pete and I went to our favorite local tavern, Barnaby's, for our usual date night. We'd not missed a Friday in months unless we were traveling. This bar/restaurant has a comfortable atmosphere, featuring a huge glossy oval wood bar where we enjoy the feeling that here, most everyone "knows our name" (well, at least the bartenders). Bar stools are always readily found in the main bar where Mark, our favorite bartender, pours our first pints before we even have a chance to sit down. On this particular night however, the place was packed! We had never seen so many folks crammed into the main bar area. We thought about leaving immediately because it appeared impossible to get a seat.

Pete and I looked at each other and shrugged. It was a 15-minute drive back home and—well, to be honest, we were thirsty. Not to totally strike out for the evening, we ventured upstairs to the second level that houses another bar and dance floor. We seldom visit the upstairs area because nothing much happens there until after 9 p.m. when the DJ spins for the mostly under 40 crowd. As it was a bit past 6, we hoped we would have more success finding a seat to grab a beer and a bite to eat. Totally vexed about our situation, we made our way up the creaky flight of wooden steps to find the cavernous bar on the second floor totally—empty.

Surprisingly, we didn't see a soul around save for the young, adorable female bartender Mandy* who seemed grateful for the company. We found the large bar area dark and unusually quiet when we took our seats. We felt kind of silly sitting by ourselves and figured we'd have a quick dinner before heading home. Because the place is essentially a "sports bar," Pete and I glanced up at the multiple television sets surrounding the room but quickly lost interest. They all appeared to be on mute anyway.

Rather pitifully, Pete and I sat there alone drinking our Blue Moon and Miller Lite looking at each other trying to make the most of our lonely "date night." After finishing our first beers, Pete asked, "Want to eat something up here or call it a night?"

"How 'bout going downstairs to see if it's opened up any?" I replied, hoping we could leave this tomblike atmosphere.

"You got it," said Pete hopping off his stool. Not two minutes later, he was back saying, "Nope, it's still packed." Bemused, I asked out loud what in the world had brought in all those people. Pete sat back down letting Mandy know we needed two menus and another beer for each of us.

As we sipped on our beers, I glanced up more and more at the four televisions directly facing me. It was unusual all the televisions in the entire room were on mute and had all been turned on to the same station as if it were Super Bowl Sunday. Something kept making me look at the screens, one and then the other, and then another. Something was certainly "off," but it wasn't just the volume. "What is it?" I asked myself. I looked around at Pete, before turning again to see Mandy still standing alone propped up against the bar. Becoming increasingly aware not one person had come up to join us, my thoughts were churning. Something eerie seemed to be happening, adding to my feeling I was missing something important.

And then it dawned on me.

Looking slowly around the room, there was no mistaking what was being televised—on every single set.

Of course, it being Friday Nov. 5, an important sporting event was taking place at this exact moment. Well, important if you are a horse racing fan.

With delight in my eyes, I turned to look at Pete. "Do you notice anything unusual on the TVs?"

Pete looked at each set curiously, catching on fast. On every screen we saw horses, race horses! It was the Breeders' Cup races; the same event that had prevented me from attending my Uncle Bob's funeral.

Pete was amazed. Neither of us could ever remember Barnabys' showing horse racing events on its screens. What's more, we probably would not have noticed this phenomenon if it weren't for the fact we were drinking alone at the upstairs bar, which is most often closed in early evening.

Pete and I grinned at each other.

We said almost together, "Hello Uncle Bob!" firmly believing he was sending a sign letting us know via live television he was "OK", and not only "OK" but, best of all—apparently, there is horse racing in heaven!

We raised our glasses toasting Uncle Bob, finding the whole situation one more "coincidence" to add to a list I was now keeping track of on my laptop. We sat there for quite a while absorbing the surreal moment. After one more salute, Pete and I left the upstairs bar to head home. We descended the old wooden steps to the first floor, and lo and behold, empty bar stools were now plentiful.

In all these years since, we have yet to see another horse race televised at our favorite watering hole.

Our evening turned out to be an enjoyable "date night" filled with reflection and remembrance. What we didn't know at the time was that in a short while, our lives would be turned upside down. We soon found ourselves faced with tough decisions and compounding loss, ultimately testing the strong foundation of my personal faith in a loving God.

CHAPTER 6

Stormy Weather

My sister Lisa lived an extraordinary life. Smart, funny, and willful she determinedly lived life on her own terms for as long as possible. While battling MS, Lisa stayed with my parents as long as she could manage safely. Standing six feet tall, her declining mobility meant she needed additional help for all the necessary activities of her day. My parents' home had small bathrooms and hallways, adding to her difficulty of navigating easily around their house. Fiercely pragmatic, she knew she needed alternative living arrangements. Despising the thought of going into a nursing home, she reached out to her friends for help instead.

Quickly, Lisa hoped she had found a solution. Her longtime friend Deanna* offered a place for her in her spacious home in Knoxville, Tennessee. Unfortunately, Lisa's dog, Barnaby, was not invited (a situation which thrilled my father who thought of the miniature Schnauzer as more his pet than Lisa's). Lisa moved in with Deanna, taking little with her. Sadly, the living arrangements proved to be short term. Once again, my sister had to search for another solution. Her physical strength was rapidly deteriorating by this time. I'm sure she must have been fearful about her future.

And then, a true angel on earth appeared in the form of a previous co-worker of Lisa's. Her name is Phyllis. She and Lisa had worked together at Pizza Hut years before and had stayed in touch after both women left the company. It turns out, Phyllis' decision to rescue Lisa ended up rescuing them both. Phyllis had recently lost her father and together they turned loneliness and grief into many days filled with laughter and endless cups of coffee and cigarettes. My sister told me she smoked like a train, hoping cancer would kill her before the MS made her life totally insufferable. So far, her plan hadn't worked.

Phyllis generously offered Lisa to move into her split-level's ground floor master bedroom. Phyllis moved her bed to the large family room area so they could both have some privacy. How many folks can say they have a friend willing to become a sole caregiver for them? My sister provided the money to have Phyllis' small lower level bathroom renovated to become handicapped accessible. For many months after Lisa moved in, they had a grand time hanging out at home. Due to the advancing MS symptoms, Lisa found it rapidly more difficult to get in and out of vehicles.

I visited her in Tennessee as often as I could get the time off to drive the ten hours for our weekend visits. Despite Lisa being older by more than eight years, we had always been extremely close. She had once asked if I would consider having her move in with us. But our home is surrounded by steps going up and down. Realistically, we quickly decided it wasn't a feasible idea.

Fortunately, wonderful events happened in Lisa's life to counter the awfulness of her disease. Lisa's only daughter, Laura, made Lisa a grandmother by giving birth to a son in June 2009. Lisa expected to become a grandmother again with the birth of a granddaughter in December of 2010. Lisa relished her role as "Nana" but it became ever more apparent that the relentless pain she endured every day was making her living unbearable. Lisa tried multiple pain and anti-spasmodic medications but none gave her much relief. If anything, the pain meds wreaked havoc on her digestive system, making eating food an uncomfortable challenge.

During this same period, my husband's father, Don, was declining rapidly from his own battle with pulmonary fibrosis, a disease leading to increased respiratory problems.

During these months, it seemed all discussions with family on both sides were centered on how to care for Lisa and Don. Pete and I were more and more fearful of how we could offer help if conditions became worse for them and, God forbid, occurred at the same time.

Despite our worries, a call to action became necessary by late March when Phyllis called me. Whispering into her phone she said, "Ellen, this is Phyllis. I've got to talk to you." I could tell by the serious tone of her voice something was terribly wrong. "What's up?" I asked, though I pretty much knew as I had recently been to Tennessee to visit them.

"I can't take care of Lisa any longer," Phyllis told me in her hushed voice, afraid Lisa could overhear. "She's barely moving and I'm really having trouble getting her in and out of her bed." After absorbing what she told me I replied, "Well, Phyllis, I guess it's time to talk about a nursing home." I knew this solution was the last thing Lisa wanted, but no one else could handle the physical demands of Lisa's care. And we didn't have the money for private care in Phyllis' home. Phyllis and I hung up and I was left wondering how I could approach Lisa to figure out what to do next.

Lisa might have been physically weak but her mind remained sharp as a tack, as well as her resolve. Possessing full mental capacity, Lisa shared her own plan. It turns out, for quite some time, she had always had a plan.

No longer able to endure the excruciating pain and muscle spasms she suffered so often, Lisa called us family members in early April 2011 and said, "On May 15, thirty days from now, I am going to stop eating and drinking." She had already notified her hospice support team about her decision. She didn't ask for their thoughts on the matter. When Lisa was determined to do something, she remained resolute and unyielding. Because she had been a smoker for most of her life, she figured it would only take a couple of weeks for her to die. Two things were made abundantly clear by her: she couldn't take the pain any longer and she desired to end her suffering on her own terms.

I drove down the second week of May to be with Lisa, knowing full well this would be the last time I would see her alive. When she asked me to bring her a burger and shake from her favorite fast-food restaurant, I happily obliged. We went over notes for her memorial service which she had already carefully planned. She even gave me an invitation list for the private gathering to take place later in the fall with strict instructions to not allow our parents to include other guests. We talked for hours, her eating little of her hamburger and drinking but a few sips of her shake. Digesting foods simply caused her too much pain.

As executor of her will, I got her instructions on last bequests, which didn't take too long. Never being materialistic, Lisa owned little. My favorite memento she gave me is a mug from Disney World depicting some of Disney's most famous villains. Lisa always found the villains in Disney movies more interesting than the princesses. She even decorated her Christmas tree with Disney villain ornaments such as Cruella, Ursula, and another favorite character, the Grinch. Although never a villain herself, she loved being among strong characters in her life. I supported my sister's decision to take charge of how she was going to go out in this world and I admired her bravery, but it was tough to watch. After witnessing the gut-wrenching pain Lisa had endured for years, most of us family and friends fully supported her decision. Her physician from my hometown later commented he believed my sister "was the most heroic woman I've ever known." None of us believed God wishes for any of us to suffer interminably from uncontrollable pain. Lisa suffered through her pain stoically for years. Who could blame her if she wanted the pain to end?

After returning home from our last visit together, Lisa began executing her final wishes. She and I talked daily for the first three weeks after she stopped eating on May 15th. I found it acutely difficult to say goodbye at the end of every phone call not knowing if we would ever speak again. Fortunately, our individual faiths kept us strong and we always believed we'd be reunited again in heaven. Laughingly she told me, "You'll find me in the smoking section."

We discussed the possibility of her sending a sign. After I shared details about the previous "messages" I had experienced, Lisa told me, "I'll think on it and let you know what my sign will be." While Lisa could barely lift her head, this did not keep her from smoking one cigarette after another. Before I left her at my last visit, in the smoky haze of her bedroom, she told me she had thought of a sign.

"I'll be the first robin of spring," she declared.

I felt a bit leery about this particular choice. Robins are fairly plentiful in Pennsylvania. In fact, sometimes I find tens if not a hundred red breasted robins on my front yard when warm spring air makes its first appearance. "How could I see 'a first'"? Still, she remained firm that her sign would be in the form of a robin. I needed to go with it.

Lisa died on June 14, 2011, 30 days from the day she took her last food. She passed her last weeks with quiet dignity, taking phone calls right up until a few days before she died. What an incredibly strong woman. According to Phyllis, she "slipped away" in the early morning hours. Phyllis phoned me soon after the crematorium personnel left her home with Lisa's body, reassuring me that Lisa died peacefully. In fact, she said, my sister never appeared to be in any discomfort her entire last month. Despite Lisa falling into a coma a couple of days before she died, Phyllis remains positive she heard Lisa call out her name in a voice loud enough to wake her, just moments before she passed. But when she went in to check on her, she was already gone.

In the days following her death, the sign Lisa gave to me to look for came to mind, but since it was almost summer, I had already missed spotting her as the "first robin." Besides, I had too much to do as her executor to dwell on robin sightings.

Lisa left strict instructions specifying she wanted "no church service." Instead she asked her friend Yvonne to host an informal gathering in the fall where invitees could come to eat, drink, and sing her favorite songs like "Rocky Top" together. Her guest list changed in the months preceding her death but her list of songs and favorite poems did not.

My dad, however, had different ideas. Being a good Southern Christian father, Dad declared, "We're having a memorial service for Lisa." Since Lisa had chosen to be cremated, he was at liberty to choose when and where her service would take place. I pointed out Lisa specifically asked there be no church service but our father remained determined to give his elder daughter a proper send off. In a matter of days, Dad had Lisa's whole memorial event planned for the end of June with soloists, hymns, and a eulogy he told us unwaveringly he would deliver.

Over 150 friends, family, and members of the community of Shelbyville attended Lisa's funeral. Dad's remarks were spot on; though how he got through it without breaking down still amazes me. After her service, we held a real old-fashioned wake at my parent's home. Friends of my parents brought food. Every room of their home was filled with people who had come to help us celebrate Lisa's life. Folks didn't end up leaving until nearly midnight. When people say good naturedly to "have a party to celebrate my life after I die," surely this is the kind of party they are talking about.

After I returned to Pennsylvania, the remaining summer weeks flew by. Soon Pete, Henrik and I were back in Kentucky the week before Labor Day Monday. While Pete and I also planned on attending my 30th high school reunion, the visit's true purpose centered on checking on my parents. Perhaps it was my imagination, but my mother seemed more distracted and shorter tempered than usual during our phone calls following Lisa's passing. It seemed prudent to make another run "home" to make sure things were OK. By this time both of my parents were in their early 80s and my mother, in particular, seemed to noticeably be slowing down.

After our arrival, Pete got busy washing windows all around their house (a chore certain to cheer my mother up) while I was preoccupied preparing the meals. The five of us managed to play a few games of Hearts and watch my folks' favorite British television shows before saying goodbye again to return home.

While driving northward through Ohio, the three of us decided, spur of the moment, to make a detour to Falling Waters to see the famed Frank Lloyd Wright house in southwest Pennsylvania. As a bonus,

Pete agreed to our staying overnight at a mountain inn nestled in the Cumberland Valley called Bedford Springs Resort near the Pennsylvania Turnpike. After checking in, we were escorted through a multitude of doorways and long hallways to our accommodations. Happily, our lovely and spacious room, along with the rest of the hotel, had been updated rather recently. White rockers on our private second-level porch added a delightful homey touch.

After quickly settling in, we escaped to the comfort of the rockers, immediately noticing again an enormous white party tent set up on the front lawn. With our curiosity piqued, we wound our way back through the labyrinth of hallways to find the front desk clerk who informed us that for a reasonable cost, we could attend the hotel's Labor Day picnic starting later in the afternoon. Our ticket covered a bountiful buffet, beverages, and live music. Seeing it as a "no brainer," the three of us quickly made the unanimous decision to attend.

After changing into something which vaguely resembled resort wear, we strolled down to the great lawn to investigate the goings on. We first noticed the feast being set up under the huge awning. Not far away, we also noticed the band.

Actually, the band consisted of only one guy. Besides a guitar, the vocalist had some sort of "music box," able to provide all sorts of extra electronic sounds to make it appear as if he was one member of a multi-piece ensemble.

After stuffing our faces, the three of us made our way to snag a good seat near where the lone musician had already started playing his first set. Luckily, we found three chairs right in front of "the band." I settled in quickly, enjoying the young musician's music; thinking a lot about my sister Lisa. During her high school years in the early 1970s, she sang and played the guitar for social events around our community, even being invited to perform once at the governor's mansion in Frankfort. She had a beautiful voice in those days and I have many memories of Lisa playing and singing her favorite folk tunes so popular in the late '60s and '70s.

As the sun waned in the western sky, I worriedly watched clouds suddenly appear. These were not the puffy white clouds of lovely summer days. Quickly, these clouds grew ever increasingly dark, with menacing hues of gray and black overtaking the evening sky. With thunder heard rolling in the distance, the three of us knew we needed to move indoors soon to safety. Despite my intense fear of lightning storms, I hated leaving our intimate concert. Music has always been therapy to me and I relished both the mountain air and the relaxing music soothing my frayed nerves. The three of us decided to stay for "just one more song" even as the skies grew more and more unsettled. The singer, appearing oblivious to the changing weather, continued to play his guitar with electronic drums providing a great background beat.

As he began to sing his last song, my heart instantly quickened. I knew this tune well. In fact, I could sing it word for word despite not having it heard played publicly in at least 25 years.

The song, "Leaving on a Jet Plane," has always been one of my favorites. It had definitely been one of Lisa's too as she had sung it a hundred times or more during my childhood.

So many years later, hearing this song performed again left me wide eyed and open mouthed. With each stanza, my heart beat faster; my spirits lifting enormously. I couldn't help but smile because I knew this song had to be a sign from my sister Lisa. Using "our song" from our childhoods, she let me know she was right there with me this evening, even as the thunder rolled and lightning flashed in the distance. Why am I so sure? One huge reason; I hadn't heard this particular song played in public in decades. What were the odds of hearing "Leaving on a Jet Plane" here, especially when I had been thinking so much about my sister and missing her terribly?

I looked at Pete. Looking at my smile and glistening eyes, he caught on fast. I didn't have to explain a thing. He could read it on my face.

Interpreting this as no coincidence, I considered this moment as Lisa's message to me signaling she was singing once again while strumming on her own "heavenly" guitar, on a stage where only peace and beauty exist. Remembering Lisa and "jet planes" gives me such comfort almost a decade later, along with remembrances of giant white party tents and rolling thunder.

Her story doesn't end here because I still had the first robin to keep an eye out for with spring's arrival the following year.

Turns out, three unusual occurrences involving robins made sure I continued to remember my sister, even tangibly feeling her spiritual presence one summer afternoon.

The first happened on a warm spring morning the year after Lisa died. After seeing the mailman's truck pull away, I put on some shoes to jog up to the mailbox located at the top of two flights of steps. As I opened the door, I stopped short after immediately noticing a big copper-breasted robin standing directly in front of me. Though this had not been my first sighting of a robin that year, I couldn't help but stare at this particular bird because *it* seemed to be staring right back at me. With our eyes locked on each other, the bird deliberately hopped toward me—yes, toward me. Finally stopping within six feet of me, the robin gazed at me a bit longer. What more could I do but say with a big smile, "Hey Lisa!"? After retrieving my mail, I told Pete that Lisa had finally come to say "hey" in the form of her designated sign, giving us both a good chuckle.

The second robin sighting happened during the same summer when my folks said that of all the odd things, a robin had built her nest less than 10 feet from their back door, eye level with the stoop; making it easy for her to be watched over. Mama robin used the crook of the downspout as the support for her nest where her babies were hatched. At first, my parents seemed a bit bewildered a mama robin would build her nest so close to human movement. After I told them about Lisa's "sign" of coming back as a robin, they became convinced and found delight in this robin. My grieving parents received solace thinking that Lisa's spirit was visiting them, albeit in avian form.

Interestingly, mama robin only built her nest there this one time.

The third odd occurrence involving a robin happened rather recently, eight years after Lisa's death.

The unusual event took place outside our home in Wallingford. My kitchen bay window looks out over the paved driveway, which gently curves down about a hundred feet to the main road. Along one side of the driveway is a long row of assorted day lilies. Gifted by my mother years before, the individual plants were personally dug up from her garden and transported to Pennsylvania. Nineteen years later, the red, orange, pink and yellow lilies have multiplied bountifully. They continue to provide amazing color and many fond remembrances of my mother and her wonderful gardening skills.

I'm not sure what made me look out the window on this particular summer day of 2019. Oddly, I noticed movement at the edge of the driveway right under a bright yellow lily's sprawling leaves. Though subtle, I definitely detected something moving about on the ground. Slipping on my sneakers, I went outside to investigate.

And there, sitting quietly at first, I discovered a full-grown robin. As I inched closer, the poor thing tried desperately to fly or at least move away from me. Sadly, I noticed the bird appeared maimed in such a way it could only hop a bit. Worse still, it was struggling terribly in the heat of the afternoon sun. While I was trying to figure out what to do, the robin suddenly stopped thrashing around. Appearing completely exhausted, it sat there on the ground, still on its little feet, eyes and beak open, its little chest heaving with each breath.

With the afternoon sun beating down on the helpless bird, something needed to be done, and soon! After digging around in the recycling bin, I found a lid from a glass jar and filled it with cool water from the nearby hose. Setting the lid on the ground in front of the bird's beak, my robin friend immediately drank greedily. Seeing the bird swallow the cool liquid gave me hope. Looking around I wondered what more could I do.

I put gloves on before picking up the now quiet bird, letting it rest in the palm of my protected hand. The robin remained quiet, allowing me to gently stroke its back while appearing to rest. A few minutes passed. Eventually, I returned the robin to the shade of the lily leaves where I hoped it would continue to recover from an injury I could not ascertain.

Unfortunately, the robin died not long after our encounter. The whole incident shook me. Initially upon seeing the robin in its distress, I couldn't help but remember my sister and her chosen sign. How bizarre the whole incident seemed, especially the bird allowing me to hold it. Was this encounter some kind of message? Another sign or a continuing weird coincidence?

The robin and my sister had both bravely endured their own measure of suffering before dying. As unfair as it is, it appears that sometimes, suffering simply has to be a part of living, and dying. Suffering; a dreaded word. After Lisa died in June 2011, I hoped I would never be asked to watch anyone struggle in a life-or-death situation again. Little did I know it would be only weeks before God asked me to walk beside someone else into the shadowy depths of a life near its end. Unbelievably, this particular someone had caused me and my family a great deal of pain. With my faith in a loving God tested to its core, I found myself forced to discover what thin lines exist between hopelessness and hope, grudges and forgiveness, hate and love.

CHAPTER 7

Moth

During much of the time my sister was struggling with the increasing challenges caused by her illness, my father in law, Don, experienced his own decline from symptoms of pulmonary fibrosis. This disease is mainly characterized by lung tissue becoming progressively damaged from scarring, making it increasingly difficult to breath. An avid snow skier all of his adult life and a fitness junkie, Don had enjoyed overall good health for most of his adult years. This all changed after being diagnosed with the respiratory disease soon after his 80th birthday. On the afternoon he received his definitive diagnosis, Don phoned my husband, Pete, declaring matter-of-factly, "I'm calling all of you boys to let you know I am dying." And that was that. He didn't elaborate too much except to explain that he had just received the diagnosis of pulmonary fibrosis which he firmly believed would ultimately end his life. An engineer of strong German heritage, Don thoroughly enjoyed creating extremely organized action plans. With great diligence, he got busy writing a guideline for his final days on earth. Putting his plans to paper, he stuck with his decisions, hardly ever deviating (even when he might be wrong). Unfortunately, all his planning didn't work out as hoped. He possibly forgot the fact that ultimately, we humans usually don't have the final say.

My relationship with my father in law can best be described as complicated. First of all, he loved telling sexist jokes, which made me wonder at times how I could have married his son. While both of us enjoyed a good debate, as the years rolled by, our differences of opinion caused increasing friction. If he didn't like or agree with something I said, he would wag his long bony finger at me telling me in no uncertain terms "No, you're wrong." Sometimes after getting so angry at me, he stormed out of the room to go cool off. Since he was such a male chauvinist with antiquated ideas about how women should think, it became easier and easier for me to antagonize him. I certainly would not have chosen to spend time with him except he was my husband's father and my two sons' grandfather. In contrast to my relationship with him, he absolutely adored spending time with his three sons and grandchildren. Unfortunately, being with his three daughters in law (and one ex) was another story.

Don and his wife, Alice, enjoyed a comfortable retirement. When they knew their traveling days were winding down, they made arrangements to host Don's 80th birthday in Florida. Everyone in the immediate family was invited except for the daughters in law (we were told we were "excused" from the event). Not being included hardly bothered me because it meant I would have some time for myself while Pete and our sons enjoyed a week away. They had a marvelous time and frankly, so did I. With this trip being such a success, Don and Alice planned a second vacation, this time telling us daughters in law we were not excused but downright not invited. Unfortunately, we ladies weren't the only ones left off the guest list. As it played out, Don seemingly appeared to intentionally exclude his youngest son (my husband) from attending the "family" trip.

He had gone too far this time!

Don called Pete in October of 2007 declaring, "I'm taking everyone on a cruise to the Caribbean next year." Then he followed up with, "The wives are not invited" (except for Alice, his wife of course). Proudly he announced, "Your mother and I are springing for the whole trip!" Having already made a big deposit, he went on to give the dates of the fabulous sounding getaway. Pete immediately looked at his calendar. Despite the cruise still being months away, my husband determined he had a work conflict during the same time as the sailing. Pete explained to his father, "Dad, I'm in the middle of a big project the week of the cruise. I can't go. Any chance it can be moved to a different week?" I'm not sure what Don said to Pete, but he made it clear he wasn't changing the date of the cruise. He did tell Pete, "You can send the boys (meaning our two teenage sons) anyway." When Pete told me what his father proposed, I stared at him in disbelief. Even Pete couldn't grasp that apparently no effort was going to be made to change the cruise date so that he could attend along with our two sons. We certainly weren't going to send our sons off to share a room alone together. After all, at the time they were barely seventeen and fourteen years of age. When my brother in law described in detail the private deluxe suite his father reserved for him, I had reached my personal boiling point.

It became quite ugly. I reached out to other family members for support in getting the date of the cruise changed. Pete and I felt devastated to find out no one seemed the slightest concerned if our branch of the family got left out of the amazing "family" trip. Bewildered, Pete and I drove over to visit his parents one more time letting them know how hurt we felt by their purposeful exclusion. They said little. Don ultimately canceled the cruise days before Christmas but the damage had been done. The separate families went into radio silence. For the following months, none of us spoke to each other.

By June 2008, relations improved somewhat when Phil and his cousin Claire had their respective high school graduation parties. Things remained strained but as an extended family we enjoyed a few civil gatherings during the summer. As the year progressed, Don became more and more symptomatic with the fibrosis, getting short of breath more easily. As 2009 rolled on, Pete visited his parents occasionally but I rarely joined him. My presence seemed to aggravate Don, and in all honesty, it was a mutual feeling. In his last ten years of life, I said little he could agree with and he seemed to love picking a fight with me over the littlest things, while continuing to wag his long bony finger at me. I felt bad I wasn't visiting Alice but even she had started saying little during my visits, preferring instead to stay in her bedroom. It turns out there was more to her reclusive behavior that would become clearer in the coming months.

At least Don remained devoted to my sons, always supporting them and their achievements.

The fibrosis relentlessly diminished Don's lung function and by the spring of 2011, he was literally homebound, attached to an oxygen tank around the clock. Henrik saw his grandfather for the last time on his prom night in late April when he brought his date, Emily*, to Don and Alice's house so Don could see for himself the great looking couple. Looking stunning in her long red dress, Emily literally took Don's breath away. Soon after the young couple departed, Don experienced a mild respiratory event keeping him virtually immobile in his upright lounge chair for the next couple of days.

Being so sure his death was imminent, Don made arrangements for hospice care not long after receiving his diagnosis. Until this point, the hospice nurse's duties seemed more or less to provide company for Don instead of true medical care. Don appeared to enjoy phoning the nurse assigned to his case, often. Quite often. He made a point on several occasions to boast how they had become "big buddies." However, as the summer of 2011 approached, Don complained that his favorite nurse, Peggy*, no longer returned his phone calls or visited as often as he wanted. This news didn't surprise me.

Despite our tenuous relationship, he and I enjoyed a lengthy discussion about religion, his belief in God, and thoughts about the afterlife around the time when he permanently took to a hospital bed in one of the back bedrooms in his home. His faith seemed to have taken him through all kinds of twists and turns in the years I knew him. Don visited numerous churches representing all types of faiths. He ultimately declared himself "a true interfaith believer." From what I could surmise, Don "transfigured" his religious beliefs into something more or less custom made for himself. During our chats about faith and end-of-life issues, Don never expressed a fear of dying. More terrifying to him was *how* he was going to die. He minced no words about his desire to go out of this world on his own terms.

In my opinion, this was a bold move.

So convinced God would take him one night while he slept, Don remained firm about his decision to stay in his home. He emphatically said "*no*" to nursing homes and hospitals even though he knew his lung condition would only worsen in the coming months.

Unfortunately, things didn't work out quite the way he had planned.

On a late July evening in 2011, I received a phone call from Don's night aide, Bernice*, working the 7 p.m. to 7 a.m. shift in his home. With Don desiring to stay in his house until he was "carried out in a box," he spent thousands every month for the in-home care he required. The small group of caregivers employed through a local agency stayed with him around the clock, rotating in twelve-hour shifts. Their duties were relatively light: fixing simple meals for him and Alice, making sure Don got his meds on time, and helping with his daily personal care. Each woman arrived daily for her twelve-hour shift beginning at 7, morning or evening. Despite their now being married now for 60 years, I never once saw Alice with Don back in his bedroom. She preferred to stay in her own room with the door closed most of the time, even as Don's condition continued to worsen.

On the evening of July 28, 2011, a perfect storm of all things that could go wrong did go wrong. I went to bed at my usual time around 10:30 p.m. falling asleep immediately. Just after 11, the ominous sound of the bedside landline phone woke me with a start. At this time of night, the ring could only mean something terrible had happened. With dread, I answered hesitantly, "Hello?" It was Don's aide. Sure enough, the news wasn't good.

"Mrs. Oetinger, this is Bernice. I'm with Don tonight. I got him up to the toilet and he's having a real hard time catching his breath. I can't get him back to bed. Can you come help me?" With Don's hospice nurse apparently not available, Bernice was obviously going down an emergency contact list I didn't know existed. I got the call with Pete away on a business trip; the eldest brother, Jim, home recovering from surgery; and the middle brother, Tom, too far away to help.

Suddenly wide awake, with dread in my heart, I reassured the frightened sounding aide, "Of course, Bernice, I'll be there as soon as I can." Looking up to God, I must have asked, "Really God? Really?" After throwing on some clothes, I jumped in my car, driving the three miles filled with anxiety. With over 26 years of nursing experience at the time, I knew whatever the situation I was going to walk into, it most definitely would not be pleasant.

What happened over the next 48 hours will stay indelibly burned in my memory for the rest of my life.

I found Don still seated approximately six feet from his bed in full respiratory distress. Not only did he suffer the embarrassment of seeing me while he was nude from the waist below, he appeared to be suffering his worst nightmare; not being able to breathe. Being claustrophobic, he had verbalized more than once nothing terrified him more than feeling like he couldn't get air. By the wild look in his eyes and the sweat on his forehead, it was obvious that he was experiencing his worst fear.

He needed help, fast!

I knew it vital that he get his breathing quickly under control. "Don," I tried to say calmly while pulling up a chair next to him. "I'm here. You're going to be OK." He sat there on the uncomfortable plastic seat of his bedside commode, gasping for each breath while keeping his eyes cast toward the floor. Quickly, I said, "C'mon we'll do this together. Let's try to slow your breathing." Putting a hand on his arm, I continued to try to talk Don "down" from his extremely agitated state. After covering his lower half, we continued on, both of us trying to get his breathing into a more relaxed rhythm.

"OK Don, try to take a breath in like this (me taking in my own deep breath). Ok, now blow out. Purse your lips and blow out as slowly as possible." I demonstrated by pursing my own lips while exhaling. "That's it. Again, big breath in—now, breathe out." For the longest while, Don continued to pant as if he was running a marathon; his chest heaving in and out.

We continued on together with me demonstrating over and over and saying as calmly as possible, "Let's try to slow it down. C'mon on. Big breath in.

Make your lips small, blow out. You're doing great. I'm not going to leave you. You've got this. Big breath in, breathe out." After repeating this countless times, he finally appeared to be in control of his own breathing.

All in all, it took well over two hours to see him relaxed enough so he could slowly walk with help back to his bed from the commode. Standing 6'4" but now weighing less than 175 pounds, his cooperation made Bernice's and my job easier. Once there, Don's legs were lifted onto his twin hospital bed, his head elevated as high as it could go, and his oxygen tube placed back to his nose. With all three of us exhausted, Don's breathing continued more rapidly than normal but, thankfully, he no longer looked like he might have a heart attack as well. I'll never forget the look on his face as he endured the excruciating agony of trying to get his breath. His eyes conveyed what appeared to be deep humiliation over being in such a vulnerable state in my presence, but I'd like to say I also saw—gratitude? Don had always been the one who liked to be in control. I'm pretty sure that of all the people in the world, I was the last person he thought he would see at his bedside during a crisis. The feeling was mutual.

When he seemed to be resting well enough, I placed a call to his hospice nurse assuming she might offer to run right over to relieve me. I phoned her around 2 a.m. but when she answered, to my astonishment, she made it clear she was not coming to check on Don. All she said to me was, "Keep giving him his medications until he is comfortable." Her orders certainly seemed vague but not knowing what else to do, I got busy locating and organizing the medications she told me should be somewhere in the house. Bernice helped me find the three most needed medicines, one of which was in the kitchen cabinet with the vitamins. Since the hospice nurse seemed to feel I could take charge of the situation, I got busy reading the directions on all three bottles knowing Don could go back into distress at any moment.

My instincts proved correct.

The crisis resumed. As Don's agitated state increased, I administered drops of morphine, alternating with Haldol and Ativan; all drugs invented for the purpose of alleviating pain, anxiety, and respiratory difficulty but not necessarily designed to be given all together for obvious lethal reasons. The hospice nurse casually instructed me to give Don whatever it took to help him breathe easier. I definitely looked up to God beseechingly, shouting in my head, "Why me, God? Why me?" Frustratingly, nothing seemed to work! I couldn't fathom how he tolerated ingesting large amounts of meds without getting relief. Then I remembered he had been using a narcotic patch for many, many months prior to this event. His breathing continued in a much too rapid and thin pattern; his chest continued to heave with his efforts. Just when I started to feel desperate around 4 a.m., Don finally appeared to rest quietly, his breathing now steady and regular. In a daze, I stayed a while longer before finally heading home to get some much-needed sleep. The crisis appeared to be resolved—for then. While driving home, I knew in my heart that this period of calm would most certainly be too brief.

My head seemed to have just hit the pillow when the phone rang again at 7:30. It was Bernice's relief aide, Fannie*, who had just arrived for the start of the twelve-hour day shift. Once again wide awake and restless, Don was struggling, not able to catch his breath. I'm sure I must have groaned once more, cursing my luck for being the only family member available. As frustrated as I was, I could not ignore Fannie's plea for help. I definitely remember asking God again, "You really are making me do this?"

Running on automatic, I drove back to Don and Alice's to find the situation even graver.

Dismayed, I immediately surmised that Don was back in the throes of finding it quite difficult to breathe. I quickly administered more of his medication. Thankfully, the drugs worked fast. In a short while, Don's breathing pattern returned to his near normal. Unfortunately, other problems became apparent. Don had soiled himself, making a bath and bed change necessary. His less responsive state was a blessing while he endured the indignity of being changed into a fresh gown and linens with the help of his aide and daughter in law. I felt so grateful for Fannie's help. She and I worked well together, coping with what needed to be done as best we could. Still, during this whole time, I couldn't believe it was all happening. And selfishly, I kept wondering, "Why me?"

By mid-morning, I went in to see Alice, who had remained holed up in her bedroom during both episodes. Gently, I explained to her she may want to go in and be with her husband as I was pretty certain we were watching an end-of-life situation unfold. She got up slowly from her recliner and used her walker to scoot into Don's bedroom. After standing at his bedside for a brief moment, she said, "I'm going to go make him some eggs." Totally bewildered, I watched her trot off to her kitchen to make Don breakfast though it was obvious to me, that Don was in no shape to eat anything, much less a scrambled egg. Deciding to "go with the flow" though, I reassured her that making eggs sounded like a great idea. Wordlessly, she began beating two eggs in a small mixing bowl while waiting for the skillet to heat up.

Of course, Don didn't eat anything but he remained calm for the remainder of the morning. He looked at me when I spoke to him but otherwise, he appeared to rest comfortably. Once again, I returned home, immediately calling Pete to fill him in on what had occurred through the previous night and into the morning. He told me his plane would land midafternoon, much to my relief. Though I felt completely wrung out from the ordeal, I felt especially sad for Don. He and I didn't have a loving relationship but I found it painful to see him suffer so much.

When Don's relief weekend hospice nurse came to evaluate him midafternoon on July 30, she took one look at him before saying, "He needs to go to the hospital and now!" Unsurprisingly, Don needed more medical attention than was possible at home. The nurse quickly made arrangements for him to be transported by ambulance. Don was not alert but didn't look to be in any discomfort.

Alice showed no interest in accompanying Don in the ambulance. She also declined our offer to drive her to the hospital later that evening. Pete and I planned to head over after grabbing a quick bite to eat. None of us had eaten much all day. Receiving no word from anyone at the hospital, we figured we had a bit of time before checking on Don.

Unfortunately, we arrived minutes too late. When Pete and I walked up to the nurses' desk to inquire where to find his father, I knew instinctively by the look on the nurse's face things weren't good. Slowly, filled with trepidation, we walked together to Don's assigned room. Upon opening the door, we discovered Don with his head extended back turned to one side, mouth wide open, and his eyes closed. He had obviously already passed away. I then spotted a figure sitting alone in the darkened corner at the other end of Don's private room. A bit startled, I realized that the visitor was our church's Associate Pastor, Rob. We hadn't realized that he had been alerted to Don being admitted to the hospital. Sadly, Rob said he too, arrived moments after Don took his last breath.

Don had died alone. Regrettably, none of his final hours had gone according to his carefully laid plans.

I could tell Don had struggled for his breath right to the end. If I felt anything at the moment it was numbness and simple relief that Don's earthly struggles were finally over. Little did I know however, my inner conflicts surrounding our relationship had yet to be resolved or that the process would take years.

The whole ordeal left me deeply shaken. It seemed unbelievable and a bit unfair that circumstances put me with him during those awful last hours. I'm 100% sure if Don could have chosen anyone in the world to be with him during his last days, witnessing his return to an infantile state (naked and unable to control his body functions), he most definitely wouldn't have chosen me.

When I asked my minister what her thoughts were about God putting me with Don for our terrible night together (she was quite aware of our stormy relationship), she answered with a reassuring smile, "It had to be you, Ellen. It had to be you." Deep down, I knew she was right when she said those words though it would take the writing of this chapter for me to fully articulate the possible reason. Almost a decade later, I think I may know the answer. God put us together to force us to reconcile the feelings that had driven us apart; my loathing of his old-fashioned male chauvinistic ways and his apparent lack of respect for me as a woman. It's certainly too late to speak for Don. All I know and believe is God was with me that night, giving me strength and the presence of mind to help as best I could. Despite asking God once or twice (or more) "Why me?", magically all the ill will locked up in my heart seemed to vanish during that time when Don needed my help the most. Love replaced hate during those hours, fear seemed to give way to hope. Remembering the power of God's love so present during our time together still rocks me to my core today.

Besides receiving the comforting reassurance from my pastor, apparent signs began appearing soon after Don died. Pete believes to this day the following signs or more accurately "messages" in his case were certainly from his dad. To ensure Pete would pay attention, his dad found a perfect host to let his youngest son know his father still had something more to say.

The first sighting occurred several days after Don passed. Pete took it upon himself to start clearing out his father's study. Don had been a highly organized man. In his office, everything had its place. There was little clutter on his desk and his file cabinet was full of carefully labeled records of 60 years of marriage, work, and family life. While examining one of many files, he noticed a large brown moth sitting on the carpet near his dad's computer desk. Despite all the stir Pete was creating in the small room, the moth didn't move. Pete said he walked over to make sure it was alive. Yep, it was definitely alive. As Pete got more curious and crept closer to the insect, the moth flinched, but only a bit. Apparently unafraid of Pete, this moth seemed quite comfortable keeping an eye on things, or perhaps, trying to supervise?

Pete told me he was sure it was his dad, relating the sighting to a similar experience he shared with his father years before. He was helping his dad clean out some stuff from his garage when they suddenly both noticed a moth sitting on the garage floor. Not moving, it apparently seemed content to monitor their work. After noticing the moth, his dad said to him, "That's Grandpa Willard watching over us." (Grandpa Willard was Pete's grandfather, who had died when Pete was a young boy). Taken with the notion the moth might be his visiting grandfather, Pete said he took a photograph of the moth. The photo has been in his archive of thousands of photographs taken over the past 40 or so years. (Oddly enough, Pete was recently able to easily locate the decades old photograph, almost as if it *wanted* to be found). Pete had forgotten about the moth sighting until he saw this one on the floor of his father's study days after his dad passed away.

We found the story of the office moth interesting but didn't give it much thought. Until again, Pete had another "visit" within the same week while riding the train.

Since Wallingford is a relatively close suburb of Philadelphia, Pete rode the regional train to and from work in the city for the 14 years he worked in the downtown office of Rohm and Haas. Folks in the neighborhood said they knew the time of day when seeing Pete walk by their house because he kept to the exact same train timetable every working day. A man of consistency, Pete always chose a window seat, allowing him to rest his head on the glass of the window. On this particular day after walking home from the station, Pete immediately sought me out telling me something pretty wild had just happened on the train ride home.

"I got into my usual seat by the window and was about to close my eyes for my quick twenty-minute nap. All of a sudden, something "big" caught my attention. I sat up and looked more closely and couldn't believe what I was seeing. I've certainly never seen anything like that before," he exclaimed.

"It was a huge brown moth." Pete declared, looking at me as if I should know the hidden meaning immediately.

Pete went on to describe the insect as having, "eyes" on each wing, a long fuzzy light brown body, and long legs appearing to cling to the glass of the speeding train. Even more startling Pete went on to say, "It definitely seemed to be watching me. It finally flew off but it sure got my attention."

Pete joked the moth must have been "Dad," there to remind him to keep an eye out on his mother, dealing poorly at the time with widowhood. We laughed together but didn't give "Dad the Moth" another thought; until another moth sighting occurred a short time later. Apparently, we weren't paying enough attention to our signs.

As the summer months progressed after Don's passing, Pete's mother, Alice, found living alone in her three-bedroom rancher a struggle. She had never lived alone in her life. When Hurricane Irene blew through the Philadelphia area, knocking down trees and power lines on the very day it would have been Don and Alice's 61st wedding anniversary, the storm was the last straw for Alice's coping skills.

It wasn't long before her sons decided it was time for her to move to a nearby assisted living facility where they hoped she might feel safer. Fortunately, because of Don's careful planning, Alice had already toured several of the facilities before he died. Alice made her choice quickly and appeared excited to move into a smaller "home" with staff available to help her when she might need assistance.

Pete had more time than his brothers to help with his mother's move and make minor cosmetic improvements on the home before putting it on the market. Daily for several weeks, he painted, repaired, and cleaned out years of accumulation filling the rooms of the moderate sized home. His brothers Jim and Tom, gathered for the final division of furniture they chose to keep, donate to Goodwill, or dispose of with one of those "I Pick Up Junk" companies. In no time, Alice's Realtor planted a "For Sale" sign in the front yard.

One afternoon in the early spring of 2012, Pete had to make an unplanned stop at his parents' house. He had forgotten his own key to open the side door but knew he could use the extra kept hidden between two bricks in the pachysandra to the left of the stoop. Pete bent over to reach for the top brick in the ground cover to expose the key. As he lifted up the brick, something startled him. Instinctively, he drew back his hand quickly hoping he hadn't angered a bee. Upon closer examination, he stared back at what he knew had to be yet again another sign from his Dad, obviously as a reminder for Pete to continue to keep his vigilant watch over his house.

Nestled between the two bricks he found a now familiar insect. It had two "eyes" on its wings and a light brown body from which long legs stretched out across the clay. "Amazingly, the moth didn't budge even when I picked up the housekey," Pete said.

Once again, he figured "Dad" had found a clever way to remind him to keep an eye on things, particularly Alice. We laughed at the coincidence of experiencing yet another moth sighting and noted how two sightings occurred at his parents' home in separate distinct locations where the "sign" couldn't be missed. We looked forward to seeing if another moth would mysteriously appear.

But there were no more moth sightings for quite some time. We might have totally forgotten about these three individual "signs" had it not been for one more—occurring many years later but ultimately connecting them all.

Unlike the strained relationships Don maintained with his daughters in law, Henrik and his grandfather always shared a loving bond. Don had been good and generous to both our sons. Unfortunately, he didn't live long enough to see either graduate from college and start their careers.

Henrik's first job placed him with an insurance company in New Hampshire. Before we knew it, it was moving day. On a typical hot morning in late June, Pete rented a U-Haul truck to move Henrik to his new home in Dover. The three of us helped load the truck with family furniture castoffs and multiple bins of clothes, bedding, and blankets. I was thrilled to have a home for all the extra stuff "stuffed" in our storage areas.

I held my emotions in check while we did our last loading of the vehicles. Pete would drive the rental truck with Henrik following behind in the family SUV we passed on to him as one of his graduation presents.

After multiple hugs, Henrik meandered over to his car. As he walked to the drivers' side door, still sweaty from loading the last of his things, he stopped in his tracks. We noticed immediately something unusual must be happening, but what could it be? Puzzled, Pete and I walked over to discover what had caught Henrik's attention. And then, there it was— of course it was!

On Henrik's driver side mirror sat a huge moth.

Although it had been years since the last sighting, we delighted in seeing it again. The large light brown moth with big "eyes" on its outstretched wings, and long legs extending from its fuzzy brown body sat unmoving on the top of the drivers' side mirror. As before, it appeared to keep a close "eye" on the proceedings of all the hugs and farewells going on between father, mother and son.

Upon seeing the moth, Pete immediately broke out in a huge grin telling Henrik, "Gramp" (the name Don's grandchildren called him) had apparently flown in to wish him farewell and good luck. Pete then proceeded to tell Henrik of the previous times he had made an apparent "Don" sighting. Going along with this unusual but fun notion of mysticism, Henrik nodded his head in agreement breaking into a big smile himself. He too considered the moth's presence as a sign Gramp wished him well on the start of his new adventure as a working man.

Last hugs went around and finally, father and son drove away, leaving mom standing on the street waving a teary goodbye.

Many years have passed since that big day.

Henrik is doing well, still living in New Hampshire, still driving his graduation gift.

We haven't seen a large brown moth with long legs and "eyes" on its wings since the sighting on the mirror. We're hoping "Don" is finally able to rest now.

The thought gives us both comfort and a wonderful sense of peace. Don told me right before our fateful night together, "I forgive you." Not at all understanding the reason for his statement, all I could do at the time was nod a bit in stunned silence.

Now, almost ten years later, I finally know what to say in response.

"I forgive you too."

CHAPTER 8

The Night the House Lights Dimmed

After my sister and Don passed only weeks apart during the summer of 2011, life within our immediate family settled down for many months. Fortunately, the next year passed with no deaths in the family on either side. In fact, in the spring of 2012, three graduations made for joyous times together: Phil graduated from the University of North Dakota with a degree in Aerospace Science, Henrik graduated from high school, and I finally walked in cap and gown after earning my Bachelor's Degree in Nursing from Immaculata University.

My mother, Else (pronounced Elsa), loved her visits to Pennsylvania, making the journey at least twice yearly. For the first years she flew up to either help with the boys or to enjoy some much-deserved rest and relaxation. She enjoyed sightseeing, particularly the art museums and the local botanical gardens. Else is best described as a woman ahead of her time. She operated a successful gift shop for over twenty years while volunteering countless hours for several philanthropic organizations in Shelbyville. In her 70s she continued to impress me with her talents and intelligence by earning her Masters Gardeners certificate. She could paint, speak three languages, throw a party worthy of a Rockefeller, and adored coming up with creative ways to make people feel special. Else always expressed her opinion. Sometimes this particular trait caused a bit of friction between her and girlfriends and, in particular, her two daughters in law. But through and through, she represented the strong, modern independent woman to a tee. Sometimes a tad too much of an indomitable force, nevertheless she could always be counted on to "get the job done."

Determined to attend my college graduation in May 2012, both of my parents flew up for a long weekend visit. During our time together, it became obvious my mother's physical health was rapidly declining. Harrowing trips up and down our stairs became a true test of strength and coordination. She attended my ceremony with the use of a borrowed small wheelchair. We enjoyed a wonderful time together; however, when Pete and I dropped them off at the airport for their return home, I knew this most certainly had been her last visit to Philadelphia.

Mother's falls had begun shortly after her 60th birthday. Strolling along, she would suddenly tumble forward to the ground, more often than not onto the pavement of a sidewalk. "I'm alright!" she'd say, getting herself upright again as quickly as possible. As she aged into her 70s, her tumbles continued. Since she managed to survive each one unscathed, we joked frequently with her saying to her, "Mother, your bones must be made of concrete."

About a year after my sister died, Mother's falls increased in frequency. Dad called more and more often telling me, "Your mom took a nosedive into the bushes walking Barnaby today," or "Your mother fell headlong into the corner table getting out of her chair." By the fall of 2012, decisions had to be made. My mom could no longer continue living at home safely with Dad. The summons went out to my siblings and their spouses to gather for a family meeting in late October.

At first, we chose to ignore the question, "What should we do about Mother?" None of us children were prepared to offer having them come to live with us and they weren't going to agree to the option anyway. Their finances made it quite clear that hiring full time help in their home wasn't possible. My mother sat stone still during the meeting before quietly saying, "I've saved up enough money for me to go to a home." Reaching into the cabinet sitting next to her favorite chair, she produced her ledger book filled with years of Merrill Lynch statements carefully stacked in chronological order. Sure enough, she had an impressive nest egg. By the end of our family meeting, Dad said he would investigate each option of assisted living facilities in town. When asked how Mother felt about the potential arrangements, she quietly replied, "I just don't want to be a burden."

Over the course of the next three years, my mother lived in not one but three different "homes." As her mobility declined, it became necessary for her to be moved to a different place which fit her needs better. Eventually, because of Kentucky laws, it became necessary for her to make her final move to the same nursing home where Uncle Bob had lived out his last months. Hopeful a medication could help, Dad and I took her to several doctors for multiple tests, all proving inconclusive. With no answers, she continued her long physical decline. Fortunately, her care in each of the facilities proved to be wonderful.

With each move, Mother's strong personality softened. Her demeanor became uncharacteristically "sweet", amazing me and my siblings. One afternoon before I walked into my mother's room at the nursing home, the housekeeper said to me," Mrs. Matthews is your mother? I love your mother! She is the sweetest woman I've ever met." After clarifying she actually meant the lady in bed two, the kind housekeeper continued with more accolades. Mother took to living in the nursing home like a duck to water and for many months, she and my father enjoyed a relationship showing more love for each other than I had certainly ever witnessed before.

Again, the honeymoon couldn't last forever. Whatever affliction was making Mother more incapacitated didn't abate. By the spring 2015, Dad called me in Pennsylvania with a report. "Your mother is really slowing down Ellie Belle." While he had made this remark to me before, this time I sensed her condition had definitely changed for the worse. I made plans to fly down at the same time Christian, my mother's godson, was visiting, to help Dad with the entertaining and cooking. By this time, Dad's meals were more often than not fast-food burgers and sandwiches.

Mother spoke less and less to any of us. Her words came out haltingly as if she found it difficult to put sentences together. Nevertheless, Dad told me Mother appeared enthusiastic about Christian's impending visit. After I arrived in Kentucky, I immediately got busy putting things together for a small cocktail party to be held at Mother's facility in Christian's honor.

What a joyous time! In addition to Christian and my parents' company, Henrik took a break from his studies at Indiana University to partake in what turned out to be our last gathering together. By now, Mother could barely stand without assistance; speaking little. On that glorious day we all imagined being on the grounds of a beautiful country estate without a care in the world. We enjoyed cheese from

Denmark and a bottle of Dom Perignon, definitely a splurge. After pouring the delicious wine into a glass flute I brought from Dad's house, Mother said before raising her glass to her lips, 'I've never had Dom Perignon before," smiling coyly as she said it. And then, as she tried to raise the glass to her lips, she stopped suddenly, appearing frozen, glass suspended in her hand mid-air. Despite her best efforts, she couldn't raise her glass all the way up to her mouth. Seeing her difficulty, I helped her take small sips until she polished off her drink, while keeping a lovely smile on her face. Clearly, she seemed delighted over the simple yet elegant party. She managed a bit of cheese and cracker before declaring, "I'm ready to go back inside now."

According to my father, before Christian returned home later in the week, Christian and my mother sat together enjoying a long conversation in Danish.

We didn't know at the time this would be the last extended conversation she would ever engage in again, in any language.

When either my brothers or I visited in the next months, my mother spoke in increasingly clipped sentences. Strangely, she also appeared more interested in her TV shows, NCIS and Gunsmoke, than engaging with us. By the time of my visit to see her in mid-September 2015, she failed to show any emotion upon my arrival into her room, an ominous sign.

It wasn't that she didn't know who I was. Whatever the disease, ailment, or illness making my mother so pitiful, her memory appeared to remain intact. She remembered dates, events, addresses, phone numbers, and the times of her favorite shows on television. She always recognized all of her visitors. Each evening, she watched the clock over her sink, waiting for my father's arrival at 6. He visited my mother at least twice if not three times daily, no matter the weather.

According to Dad, Mother suffered a couple of "close calls" prior to my visit in September. One in particular still makes me chuckle.

Sometime in the early spring of 2015, Dad called saying grimly, "You better come home soon. It looks like your mother is in her last hours." Concerned, both Pete and I took off from work, making the eleven-hour car ride to Kentucky the next day and preparing for the worst.

Imagine my surprise when I found my mother sitting upright in her recliner eating a bowl of Rice Krispies. I took one look at her and said, "Wow, Mom, you don't look like you're about to die." She smiled and gave a bit of a giggle, while continuing to eat her cereal. Pete and I asked Dad to tell us "What exactly is your definition of 'last hours'? He chuckled a bit, remarking what a miraculous recovery my mother had made since his phone call.

When Dad called again, saying once more, "Your mother appears to be going downhill fast," Pete and I weren't so ready to jump in the car again. I had, after all, returned from my September visit a couple of weeks prior and could not get away easily.

Fortunately, my brother Beau said he would drive up from South Carolina to check on our mother, arriving early October. Unfortunately, this time, it appeared my father made a correct observation. Beau called me soon after he arrived to let me know, "things didn't look good." He in turn called my younger brother Bland to inform him about the situation rapidly changing. Including my father, the three men decided it would work best to take shifts sitting with Mother, who was getting more and more incoherent.

Once more, I asked God, "Really?"

After a great deal of thought, I decided to ask my brothers to sit vigil until I could arrive later in the week because I had agreed to fill-in for a coworker and we had plans to host a pre-wedding cocktail party for our friends Rik and Jennifer. Their daughter Katherine was marrying that weekend. Following a family tradition, my own mother had given this same type of party several times for the children of her good friends. Beau readily supported my decision, telling me he would keep me abreast of the situation as it played out. For all any of us knew, Mother could snap back as she had done several times before. Neither my father nor my brothers pressured me into coming home, kindly reassuring me I had already done enough for both our parents. I have to admit, I felt extremely grateful.

As the week progressed, her condition didn't improve. With each passing day, she responded less and less. We had already discussed whether or not to do aggressive treatment to temporarily improve Mother's condition. Her doctor reported to my father that possibly, medications might improve her *quantity* of days, but not her quality. None of us wanted her to suffer. Dad produced my mother's living will, The Five Wishes, making sure everyone involved in my mother's care read the details of the document describing exactly how she desired to be treated when her end of life neared. She made it clear in the legal document that she had no desire to linger or be kept alive artificially if she became gravely ill or her quality of life became poor.

Before finishing my degree in 2012, I had to plan and execute a community project. During the fall of 2011, I learned about the Five Wishes living will. Using layman's terms, this easy to follow legal document allows people to convey exactly what they want their "wishes" to be when in an end-of-life situation. Both of my parents completed their individual copies soon after my graduation during one of my many trips home. Before leaving them, I made sure my parent's physicians had a copy to place in their individual charts. Serving as her personal guidebook, Mother's Five Wishes document clearly stated that if her physicians determined her quality of life could not improve, she wanted to have comfort care measures only. Beau told me he especially appreciated having Mother's living will document to consult. Our mother had included specific acts of kindness she wanted done for her during her final days such as her hand being held, and her lips moistened periodically as she slept.

By Wednesday, I grew hopeful Mother would hold her own for a few more days.

Thursday, October 8, was not only the day of the party in Wallingford but also son Henrik's 22nd birthday. Moments after I got to work, my brother Beau called informing me our mother was struggling to breathe. In my heart, I knew it wouldn't be long. The timing still seemed improbable. Pete and I called Henrik to wish him a happy birthday, choosing not to let him know about the situation going on in Kentucky. I decided to also not say a word to Jennifer or her daughter Katherine, hoping Mother might hold on for another day. Of course, we could have canceled the party. However, I knew if I asked my mother, she would have responded, "The party must go on!"

As I had learned from my mother, I prepared for the cocktail event by pulling out all the stops. For days prior, I polished silver platters, carefully ironed the linen tablecloth, and created flower arrangements for each living area. At 6:25, five minutes before "show time," all seemed ready to go. Noting it getting more and more dark outside, I hurried to the front hall to turn on the porch lights. We expected several elderly attendees, one in particular arriving via a wheelchair, making the illumination of our front steps especially important.

Flipping "on" the switch, I looked out to make sure the lights came alive. "That's odd," I said upon seeing only darkness enveloping the entire front of our house. I tried several more times. Still no lights. "Ugh!! "This can't be happening!"

"Pete!" I shouted. "Pete, come quick! The lights aren't working! You've got to do something!" I was literally shaking in desperation. These evidently broken front lights had been gifts from my mother for Christmas a few years earlier. Until this evening, they had worked perfectly. Of all times for them to not come on!

Pete tried the switch before dashing outside to hit the reset button on the lamps themselves. Walking back into the front door, he shook his head and mumbled, "I have no idea why they aren't working. There is nothing I can do." Still frantic, I then saw our first guests making their way down our dark front stairs. Trying to put on our best welcoming (and calm) smiles, Pete and I ushered in folks now quickly streaming in one after another. No one uttered a word about the walk being so dark. Before long, our guests filled the house with laughter and charged excitement. The upcoming nuptials were happening in two more days.

Pete managed the bar while I refilled empty platters of roast beef sandwiches and heavy hors d'oeuvres. My mother taught me plenty of things:

how to make a delicious gravy with no lumps, how to make a floral centerpiece in under fifteen minutes, and luckily, how to make entertaining look easy. I grew up watching her play hostess for hundreds of dinner, cocktail, and bridge parties. During the entire evening, I thought of her often, wondering whether she could hold on for just a while longer. No one attending had any idea of what was happening back in Kentucky and I hoped to keep it that way.

Minutes after 8, the landline phone rang. Knowing with certainty the reason behind the call, I excused myself to pick up a phone away from the boisterous noise of folks apparently having a wonderful time.

"Hello?" I answered, while sitting down in my husband's favorite recliner. It was my younger brother on the phone.

"Hey Ellen, it's Bland."

"Hey Bland. What's happening?" In a hushed tone, he said, "Mother passed a few minutes ago." He filled me in on the few details quickly. I told him that I would call back shortly, explaining we still had a house full of party guests.

Later, my dad told me that before his wife of 63 years and mother to his four children slipped into unconsciousness, he told her, "I love you." With a bit of a chuckle, he relayed Mother's reply, "You better."

After I hung up, it became obvious the party had run its course. As if on cue, all our guests got up from their seats and began filing back out the door thanking us for "a wonderful time." I remember plastering a smile on my face, still not letting on that my mother had died a few moments before. At last, Jennifer and I stood together, the guests now gone.

"Jennifer, you should know. Mother passed away a few minutes ago."

"Oh Ellen, I am so sorry."

"Thanks," I continued. "Phil is driving me down early tomorrow morning. Of course, this means I won't be able to attend the wedding. But Pete is staying—work stuff—so he'll be able to make it."

"We're going to miss you but of course, I understand." Jennifer gave me a much-needed hug. Waving to my men, she said "thank-you" and "goodnight" before disappearing into the darkness.

After everyone left, I helped clear the last of the things from the tables in the living room. Curious, I thought I would try the lights once more.

This time, like magic, both lamps shone brilliantly across the front walk. "Are you kidding me?" I said out loud to myself before yelling, "Pete, you have got to come see this!" As Pete entered the front hall, I said excitedly, "Look! They now work!" showing him with the flip of a switch how both lights now shone brightly.

"Humph," declared Pete. "That's so weird. I can't imagine why they weren't coming on before." Pete examined the lights now going on and off as he toggled the light switch up and down.

For a while we both stood there puzzled about the whole event. Of course, Pete and I came up with our own theory, attributing what had happened to being some sort of sign from my mother.

Though she had certainly still been alive at 6:30 when the lights refused to work, we kind of joked that perhaps my mother, in some sort of a state between life and death, sent a signal to us, letting us know she had no intention of missing a good party. At least, in my grief, thinking so gave me a measure of comfort. With my mother's health being so poor for so long, my feelings were definitely conflicted about her passing. Certainly, I would miss her. But she told me quite adamantly many times as she aged that she had no desire to linger. I felt grateful she hadn't "lingered" long at all once her quality of life became clearly poor.

Pete and I considered the light outage and recovery as another sign from my mother, or God perhaps. We humans can't possibly know exactly what happens in the moments before actual death occurs, right? I still get chills when I think of all the attempts I made to turn the two light fixtures on without getting the slightest blink. How incredibly weird that the lights my mother gave us remained dark during her last hours, but soon after she passed, burned steady and bright, lighting the way of a beckoning path.

Oddly, this wasn't an isolated event involving "house lights."

I remember the second sign well. With both my mother and sister now gone, I made regular trips to see my niece, Laura, who lives with her husband and five children in Nashville, Tennessee. She is my sister

Lisa's only daughter and my parent's first grandchild and only granddaughter. On two occasions, I flew alone to visit Laura and her family and to offer a bit of childcare help. With all of her kids still under the age of eight, describing our visits together as busy is a gross understatement.

With the improving weather arriving in March 2016, a few months after my mother died, I made my first trek of the year to visit my niece and her family. During this particular visit, I like to think my mother sent another "sign," signaling her desire to be remembered during our girl time.

With no quality time to talk during the day, I especially looked forward to the evenings when Laura and I would curl up in the large great room to finally have some treasured adult conversation and wine after her brood were more or less tucked in their beds. I say more or less because seldom did her children actually stay tucked in their beds. Fortunately, this evening most of her little people stayed in their rooms after saying goodnight. During our conversation, I decided to share the story about the evening her grandmother passed.

"You want to hear a crazy story about the night your grandmother died?," I asked. Her expression and body language suddenly appeared a tad guarded.

"OK?," said Laura with obvious hesitation.

Filling her in on the pre-party details, I quickly got to the fun part saying, "And when I went to turn on the front lights, they wouldn't come on. Now, mind you, I had 30 people arriving any second in the dark. Can you imagine how exasperated and upset I felt?"

"Yea, I'm sure you were," replied my niece patiently listening to her nutty aunt's story about lights and signs.

Suddenly before I could continue any further, we heard two small explosions. "Crack," "Crack! The noises seemed to come from right over our heads as the room went suddenly dark.

"Whoa, what was that?" I cried out, shooting up to a sitting position.

Startled to attention as well, Laura also sat up quickly, glancing around. She looked toward the ceiling and figured out the reason behind the disruption.

The two overhead lights above us blew out simultaneously at the exact moment I spoke of my lights not turning on during the party.

"Wow, that's really strange," Laura said before padding off to her pantry to try to find replacement bulbs and a ladder.

She found two new bulbs and together, we replaced the bulbs which had blown out, as if on cue, during the telling of my story. I remember commenting, "What are the odds of that happening?" "Laura, those lights going out now must be "Grand" (the name Laura called her grandmother) letting us know she is with us tonight. You know how much she would have liked to be included." She and I laughed together, knowing my last statement to be true.

After putting away the ladder and disposing of the burned-out bulbs, we returned to our respective sofas to resume our conversation. It seemed an appropriate time to tell Laura about other "signs" I had received over the years. Thankfully, she listened attentively being characteristically kind; not telling me I am totally off my rocker. Given the fact she is a psychiatrist, her interest is especially appreciated.

As far as I know, those bulbs are still burning brightly today.

Oh, and the front lights on my house? It's been years now, and those lights continue to shine bright— like the memories of my mother.

After returning home from my visit to see Laura, our calendar became filled with fun events such as Henrik's college graduation and a family wedding. Phil moved to the Netherlands in June ready to start his studies in Computer Science at the University of Groningen in September. I continued my visits to Kentucky to check on my father (and fill his freezer) right on through the summer months.

With both sons moved away, Pete and I actually enjoyed the quiet of an empty house.

What we didn't know at the time was that, with the change of season in September, our inner qualities of strength, hope, and faith were going to be tested once again.

CHAPTER 9

Butterflies and a Song

My mother in law, Alice Kress Oetinger, was born in Buffalo, New York, on May 8, 1929, a few months before the stock market "crashed" and ushered in the Great Depression. When I first met Pete, he described his mother as a "piano singer." Taking his description literally, I assumed his mother made a living singing in cocktail lounges around Buffalo. I pictured her wearing flashy clothes, sparkly costume jewelry, and plastering her face with lots of makeup before belting out Doris Day songs for a living. Was I ever wrong! Though she did wear "big hair" dyed "Bambi Blond," Alice turned out to be totally the opposite of what I originally believed. Pleasant and extremely quiet, Alice enjoyed listening to conversations but rarely made herself the center of attention.

A bit confused after our first dinner together, I asked Pete on the drive back to my apartment, "I thought you said your mother is a "piano singer." He looked at me kind of funny before bursting into laughter. "She *sings* at her *own* piano," he clarified, chuckling over my wrong conclusion.

I soon discovered more personal information about Alice, some of her history even surprising other family members. Despite having never finished college, she spoke and understood Spanish fluently. Astute at numbers, she always took care of the family checkbook and oversaw her and Don's retirement finances. After I married her youngest son, she humbly confided that in addition to being a class yearbook editor, she had also graduated as her high school class valedictorian. When she told me all this, I am sure my eyes conveyed my disbelief. I only knew her to be a sweet demure lady who deferred all decisions, big and small, to her husband. Apparently feeling the need to hide her intelligence, she kept quiet during larger get togethers. Once, my father in law quipped in front of my parents that Alice could be "happy in a broom closet." Astonished at his comment, I made a vow right then and there, that no one (particularly Pete), would ever speak a similar pronouncement about me.

Alice appeared to enjoy being a wife and grandmother but she made it abundantly clear she adored spending time with her three sons the most. I think her daughters in law were more or less necessary evils in the family scheme of things. In her later years, she confided to me she didn't like women much, and trusted what men had to say more. Hence, she preferred male doctors and pastors. She and I enjoyed an amicable relationship; however, we weren't close. On the other hand, Pete cherished his "Mom," as he always called her. They enjoyed a strong bond which grew stronger as they both aged. Unfortunately, her later years and end of life proved to be a long, agonizing journey; not only for her but for Pete. Her physical and mental decline became a concern soon after Don's death. When she suddenly withdrew from activities she had enjoyed most of her life, we knew something was seriously wrong—especially when she stopped singing.

Possessing many gifts, Alice loved singing the most. As a contralto, she sang professionally in choirs and for weddings during her younger years. Besides being a mother, it was in her music she seemed most happy and, to Don's credit, he supported her talent by encouraging her to take voice lessons and be active in a quartet in Buffalo and in her church choir. She took her music seriously, practicing with diligence. I didn't know it for years, but Alice was a perfectionist. She didn't do anything if she felt she couldn't do it with exactness and she seldom agreed to try anything new.

So it came as a bit of a shock when suddenly, right before her 70th birthday, Alice decided she would no longer sing. Period. This included the two local choirs she'd joined soon after moving to Pennsylvania. And that woman could be stubborn! We tried to get her to change her mind, but when Alice made a decision, she rarely changed it. She never told us why she so abruptly stopped using her vocal gifts.

At the time, we didn't know her decision to stop singing was a turning point for the rest of her days.

As Alice aged into her late 70s and early 80s, she more or less retired from life altogether. We children had vague ideas something was amiss with her behavior, but we chalked up her sudden departures from family dinners and holiday gatherings to her becoming fickle and eccentric. Mistakenly, I sometimes assumed she broke up a party as a purposeful and vengeful action to get back at us for unknown reasons. Before he became too ill, Don did all of the shopping for the both of them, even picking out Alice's library books. Still, we family members didn't think much about it. Relations certainly didn't improve much after the cruise incident but occasionally we enjoyed a few more family meals together. Increasingly, Alice stayed mute during most conversations. After Don died, we family members hoped she would come out of her shell and take part in life again. We figured "Domineering Don" had kept Alice from speaking her own mind and doing her own things all those years. We grew hopeful she would find joy in being with us; participating in activities with her grandchildren.

We soon discovered this was not to be.

Alice didn't cope well with being alone in her house and called for help often in the days after becoming a widow. Within a few months, her sons deemed it necessary for her to move out of her ranch home into an assisted living facility. Her sons consulted her on what she wanted to take with her to her new two-bedroom apartment. Preferring to live with simplicity, Alice chose to take: one twin bed, a well-worn recliner, an old desk, a post-war metal file cabinet, and an unbelievably vivid red floral sofa along with a few tables. She seemed to have little interest in anything she had possessed during her long life, including her photo albums. We chalked up her apparent lack of interest in keeping worldly possessions as her being in shock over losing her husband of 60 years. We all hoped she'd snap out of this weird fog which seemed to have settled into her brain. Unfortunately, it wasn't long before we realized this fog wasn't showing signs of lifting anytime soon and might be a symptom of something far more debilitating than we family members first imagined.

Months rolled by and Alice went in and out of mood swings and weird periods of altered mental status that everyone continued to ignore. Many times, staff found her sitting in the dining room at 4 a.m., thinking it time for breakfast. If asked, she said, "I can't read the numbers on my clock. They are too small." To try to remedy the situation, Pete installed new timepieces with bright red digital numbers throughout her apartment. One in particular had numbers so large I'm sure it could have been read by passersby walking in the hall outside her door. Still, nothing seemed to help orient her to the time of day. Her mood became increasingly sullen.

For months, our niece, Claire, and I took turns taking Alice to her frequent doctor appointments. She seemed to like the attention when the physician talked to her directly, but the upbeat feeling she exuded for him disappeared as soon as she was helped back into the car to return home. Her cognitive tests diagnosed dementia and depression but she responded poorly to any medications prescribed. In particular, antidepressants caused her to experience frightening hallucinations. She phoned Pete fairly often, complaining that she saw spiders hanging from her ceiling or, just as frightening, that she smelled smoke coming from the hallway outside her door. Her physician discontinued most of her medications in hopes these experiences would cease. Soon enough though, the hallucinations began happening without her being on any medication other than glaucoma drops and a blood pressure pill. She often said "tiny children" came to visit her, sitting on the arm of her recliner. Pete reported her "sightings" to her doctor but little could be done as she had responded so poorly to any previous treatment. She often chose to sit in her chair and sleep most of her day.

It got so she "forgot" how to use her television remote, so it stayed off. Talking on the phone became difficult as she often held the receiver upside down while saying loudly, "I can't hear you." Frustratingly, we could do little to help her as we watched her mind figuratively slip away.

Months turned into years. By 2016, Alice's nearby grandchildren moved away after completing their various educations. Pete, in his new early retirement role, visited Alice two or three times daily discovering with time Alice appeared more confused and unhappy. Alice often declared, "I'm ready to go. Everyone else is up there having a good time." She once quipped to me, "I think God has forgotten me." Her husband and beloved sisters had predeceased her now by many years, no doubt increasing her sense of feeling abandoned. Despite all the reassurances given to her to try to help her feel more appreciated and loved, she continued to become more and more despondent.

Even music stopped giving her joy. Pete bought his mother a wonderful electronic piano for her apartment hoping she might enjoy playing again. For most of her life, she spent hours at her piano playing while often singing along with the music. She especially enjoyed songs from one of her favorite musicals.

Sadly, she only tried the new piano once, giving up immediately saying "I can't play anymore." For a while, I tried playing some of the music from her books to encourage her to sing along but those efforts failed as well. Eventually, Pete tucked the piano away in Alice's storage closet along with a mountain of music. Her depression became infectious, especially to Pete who after returning from a frequent visit to check on his mother, came home morose and grumpy himself. With his bad moods now affecting our relationship, I implored Pete that something had to be changed.

As the fall 2016 approached, Pete called a meeting with his brothers as he needed a break from constantly caring for Alice as her mental status continued to decline. Thankfully, Tom, still living in Louisville, Kentucky, quickly stepped up to the plate welcoming the opportunity to help with Alice's care. Both Pennsylvania brothers quickly accepted Tom's offer with gratitude.

Before the end of August, Tom found a lovely assisted living facility in Louisville not far from his own house. Best yet, the "home" offered a memory care floor. It seemed perfect for Alice. Knowing she might again resist a change (she went on a hunger strike during a visit to Kentucky two years before when we took her there to give Pete a respite), we delayed telling her about the move. Pete and his brother Jim packed up a large suitcase with a few outfits, pajamas, a box of photos, and her much loved cosmetic case acquired maybe sometime in the 1960s.

With the upcoming car ride planned to take over eleven hours, Pete rented a minivan to afford more room and comfort for his mother while she rode in the front passenger seat and I in the second row. Something told me from the beginning this could be an agonizingly long car ride.

The big day arrived! With our own suitcases tucked in the back of the van we drove over to Alice's place on a sunny and clear day in late September. I headed to the dining room where I knew I'd find Alice enjoying her breakfast. It was her favorite meal and she always made her way to the dining room fully dressed and in a fairly good mood. Walking up to her I said, 'Hey Alice. How are you doing?" Clearly, she appeared astonished to see me but she continued to keep eating her daily order of scrambled eggs, bacon, toast, and black coffee without saying anything but a brief, 'Hello there." With Pete patiently waiting in the van, I sat with her until she polished off the last of her cup of coffee. "Mom?" I began, "Pete is waiting outside. We're going on a car ride." Momentarily surprised but agreeable, she pushed herself up from the table, put her walker in front of her, and slowly ambled with me to the van. Upon seeing us, Pete jumped out, hurrying over to the front passenger door while greeting his mother with a big "Hey Mom, it's a beautiful day for a drive." By now, Alice moved like a board and it took both Pete's and my efforts to get her seated and sitting relatively upright. After a bit of pushing and prodding, Pete buckled her safely into her seat, placed her walker into the back of the van, and threw the vehicle in gear. We were off!

Before reaching the interstate, Pete began a book on tape using the van's CD player but Alice quickly lost interest. Since it made more sense to continue in silence, the three of us settled in quietly. For the first few hundreds of miles, all appeared to be going quite smoothly. I kept busy in the back seat knitting Christmas hats for Laura's twins (her fourth pregnancy had produced an added bonus) while Pete calmly chatted occasionally "to" his mom (she engaged little in their conversations). Finally, seeing his mom appearing happier when looking out the window, he stopped with the chit chat altogether.

Bathroom and meal breaks proved quite challenging as expected. Alice refused to go into the ladies-room without a lot of coercing. To circumvent her stubborn refusal to at least go wash her hands, we convinced Alice she could only order her lunch *after* using the facilities and cleaning up. Alice attended to her needs and seemed thrilled with the McDonalds cheeseburger she ordered. To keep on schedule, we got our lunches to go and as Pete pulled back onto the interstate, he glanced at his mother only to see her eating her cheeseburger along with its paper wrapper. "Mom, don't eat the paper!," Pete cried out while trying to concentrate on the road as well. "Ellen, can you help Mom?" Seeing her indeed munching away on bits of the paper, I removed the wrapper completely leaving her with her burger to finish. Pete and I looked at each other in his rearview mirror. We both realized at this moment how much more Alice had slipped mentally in the recent weeks than we had realized.

Eleven hours into our odyssey, we finally neared our exit on the outskirts of Louisville. "Look Mom, we're almost there," Pete said enthusiastically to his mother. All in all, the trip had gone rather well. Pete and I shared a congratulatory look at each other before disaster struck. Glowing in the darkness of the night, we saw the oncoming ominous big orange sign: "Road Construction Next 5 Miles." Sure enough, traffic came to a complete and most definite stop. "So close and yet, so far away," I muttered from the back seat.

At this point, the mental glue holding Alice's coping skills together came completely undone. Suddenly, she became enraged at some imaginary object on the floor near her foot. While pointing downward, Alice spewed a stream of obscenities leaving Pete and me speechless. Neither of us could imagine her using such language. With Pete inching the car forward in sporadic feet at a time, he found it difficult to keep his eyes on the car ahead while trying to calm his mother at the same time. We found ourselves literally trapped. To make matters worse, temporary road construction signs informed us we had a torturous long four miles yet to go.

Trying to divert Alice's attention by vividly describing our family trips together in Canada, I covered topics such as, "Do you remember when all of us were up at Star Lake and your grandkids pretended they were pirates? How about when the raccoon kept knocking over the metal trash cans and Don thought he outfoxed them by putting piles of rocks on the lids but the little devils kept knocking them over, rocks and all?" I grew more and more desperate to come up with things to say which might alleviate the situation.

My attempts to help calm Alice ultimately proved futile. With our "little" car ride entering its twelfth hour, Alice's anger continued to escalate. While she vehemently yelled at an imaginary villain, Pete and I kept staring at each other in the rear mirror, both believing we could be in serious trouble. Obviously, we needed to get to our destination and soon!

A little before 9 p.m., traffic finally started moving again. We arrived at Alice's new "home" in a matter of minutes. With all three of us in a daze, Pete's brother Tom greeted us the moment we pulled up under the portico. Even more a blessing, staff from Alice's floor walked outside welcoming her with big smiles. Alice appeared more at ease immediately after arriving. She took a quick tour of her new room before we all gathered in the small dining area down the hall for a delicious pizza dinner. With Alice's odd temper tantrum forgotten, it appeared her move to Kentucky had been a success after all.

Sadly, her contentment passed quickly. Despite being well looked after, Alice's mental state continued to deteriorate even more quickly. Increasingly belligerent, she began displaying more and more angry outbursts. Once she barricaded her door with her walker and on another occasion, staff found her "hiding" under her bed (she weighed in at over two hundred pounds, so this was quite a feat). By early

November, Alice's facility director contacted Tom informing him that sadly, Alice needed more supervision and care than they could provide. Soon, Alice was transferred to a nearby psychiatric facility so she could be monitored closely.

In a matter of days, Alice stopped eating, becoming rapidly more unresponsive. A couple of years before, I helped Alice complete her own Five Wishes living will. She could still make sound decisions then and expressed exactly what she wanted when her end of days appeared to be nearing. I remember starting with the easy questions like "Do you want a funeral or a shindig after you go?" She laughed at the time telling me, "I want a family gathering like my dad had at someone's house." She didn't care whose house; she just wanted it in a home. She emphatically "wished" to be allowed to be "let go" if her heart should stop beating or she stopped breathing. I checked off the appropriate boxes for this "wish" along with her other directives. After completing her wishes, together we had her document witnessed, signed, and copied before giving her physicians a copy for her medical records. Pete and I kept a copy as well for possible reference if needed.

When Pete's brother Tom called to let him know their Mother's death appeared imminent, Pete wasted no time in purchasing a plane ticket to Louisville. I had already left for a girl's trip with my neighbor Dee and two other women for a week in Aruba, so Pete made the trip alone.

Pete arrived in time to sit with his mother with the company of Alice's granddaughter, Allison, and ex daughter-in-law, Pam. She passed away peacefully a few hours after Pete arrived.

When Pete contacted me in Aruba with the news Alice had passed away moments before, I had just sat down outside on the high upper floor terrace of the condo building. The group of us girls were enjoying a pre-dinner cocktail before walking to a favorite restaurant nearby. Because I didn't have an international phone plan, Pete texted me via Dee's phone that Alice had passed. The news of Alice's passing came as a bit of a shock because when I left for my trip Tom said her condition appeared to be stable. Obviously, things had quickly taken a turn for the worse. After returning the phone to Dee, I remember sitting there on the outside deck of the condo thanking God Alice was finally rejoined in spirit with her family and friends. She particularly looked forward to being with her sisters again, celebrating together with maybe a grand heavenly sing-a-long. While I sat quietly contemplating, my friends didn't utter a word.

Pete reassured me I needn't come home early. He and his brothers were going to sit up most of the night and reminisce around the campfire at Tom's home in the country. He told me they had already decided his Mother's memorial service would be held sometime the next year.

Sitting alone, I remembered Alice. She proved to be rather multi-faceted. While not expressive about her feelings, she found ways to make sure her family knew she loved them. Though quiet in nature, she laughed easily and sincerely. While not a gourmet cook, her chocolate chip cookies were legendary. Personifying "still waters run deep," Alice rarely expressed her emotions (which is why the episode in the car was such a shock) but her pleasure with being with her sons and grandchildren made her fun to be around before dementia took her lovely, kind spirit.

"Please God," I remember praying, "Please let Alice find some peace."

And then, almost seemingly in response to my plea, I heard something. Music? Most definitely hearing music, I sat straight up and tried to figure out the source of the tune. I quickly determined the ethereal melody was coming from the building complex on my right.

And that tune! Familiar, yet seemingly out of place, I couldn't yet put my finger on the name of the song.

Suddenly, it hit me! I knew this song, and knew it well though I hadn't heard it in years.

Becoming more excited, I asked the girls sitting on the other side of the patio, "Do you hear that?" The now familiar music continued to fill the air. Kindly, they listened and said they too could also hear music coming from somewhere but they weren't sure what the song was called.

But I was. While I could hear no one singing the words along with the melody, I knew them by heart.

This particular song from my childhood had also been a favorite of Alice's.

"Edelweiss"

We were hearing an instrumental version of Edelweiss, a hit song from the musical *The Sound of Music*.

Humming along, I knew this song had to be a sign from Alice because I remembered many occasions when Alice played this tune on her piano while singing along, alone or with Don and her sons. Pete told me over the years how he and his family had enjoyed countless sing-a-longs with his mother while standing around her baby grand. "Edelweiss" had been one of the favorites. I recalled merrily my own joining in on the song with the boys many years before.

Hearing "Edelweiss" in Aruba gave us girls cause to stop and wonder. None of us could figure out the source of the music, adding to the surrealness of the event. With a big smile, I filled my friends in on the connection between this particular song and Pete's family singalongs. Casually mentioning my history of getting signs from "beyond," they politely listened, saying the whole thing did seem a bit uncanny. I couldn't wait to get home to tell Pete all about receiving yet another apparent "sign"; this one from his mother!

Recently while writing this story, I remembered that my grandmother, "Mimi," and I must have listened to the music from Rodgers and Hammerstein's, *The Sound of Music*, a thousand times during car rides in her various Ford automobiles. She owned only this one 8 track tape, so we listened to the music during our many car rides together during my childhood.

Remembering this makes me wonder if perhaps Alice and Mimi are once again enjoying singing together in a heavenly choir. They both had beautiful soprano voices. Both had enjoyed singing professionally for weddings and funerals during their younger days. Both had been active in church choirs for decades. Thinking of them singing together gives me plenty of reasons to remember and smile.

In any case, Alice's story does not end in Aruba. Months later, shortly before her memorial gathering, Pete feels sure he too received his own personal message from his mother. It came in the form of one of nature's most lovely creatures.

Alice loved butterflies. She decorated her kitchen in Buffalo with butterfly wallpaper and wore her butterfly blouse we gave her for her 84th birthday so often, Pete bought a back-up for when one needed washing. Ever devoted to his mother, Pete often took care of the details involving his mother's care at her facility, including doing her laundry.

After she died, Pete missed his mother but also felt relief she was no longer "left behind" and had finally reunited with the family and friends who predeceased her.

In the summer of 2017, seven months after Alice passed, Pete and I traveled to Kentucky to attend my father's funeral (yes, unfortunately another family death) and visit with Tom and his wife, Judy.

Describing Tom and Judy's horse farm as bucolic is an understatement. Their property features gently rolling hills, a main house resembling a small French chateau, and plenty of acres of land to keep the various animals happy. A short walk from the main house is an inground pool with a large patio for entertaining. Tom had kindly opened the pool up for the summer shortly before our arrival. Soon after we settled in, Pete retrieved the pool strainer to collect the usual debris such as bugs and leaves before we took a cooling dip.

Skimming the top of the water, Pete suddenly called out to me, "Ellen, come here! I need to show you something." Hearing his excited voice, I quickly got up from my chair to go investigate. As I got near the pool, he yelled and pointed to his foot, "Stop!" Do you see it?" I quickly stopped in my tracks concerned something was about to bite him. Then I noticed "it." On his shoe sat a full-grown beautiful monarch butterfly. Pete grinned from ear to ear as the butterfly slowly fluttered its wings up and down, not leaving its perch for what had to be for well over a minute. With a big smile on his face, Pete declared with certainty, "It's Mom."

Watching him looking so pleased, I enthusiastically agreed with him.

This butterfly, whether only a messenger, a beautiful apparition of his mother's spirit, or maybe a symbolic gentle whisper of a motherly hug, made

Pete remember his mom as the lovely, loving, and talented woman she had always been to him.

Seeing the butterfly gave me a brief moment of comfort. After all, our purpose for being back in Kentucky was to attend my father's memorial service. I can't remember looking for a sign from him at that particular time. I still firmly believe we humans can't go asking, demanding or searching for a sign. Instead, usually without warning, they show themselves at the right time. In reality, the rest of our visit, including his service, passed without any otherworldly signs or messages.

Weeks later, Dad's sign did appear out of the blue. It was immediately recognized by the only two people left in the world who would associate him with this relic from long ago.

CHAPTER 10

The Maverick

My father, William Edmund Matthews, a.k.a. William E. or Bill, was born in Finchville, Kentucky, in the spring of 1930. He was the youngest, and most precocious from what I heard, of three boys. My personal real-life superhero, Dad possessed many attributes but one in particular singled him out to folks who knew him; his unflappable positive outlook. Dad lived his life as a true maverick, rising out of bed every day eager to take on the world.

He married my mother in 1952 because, as he told me right before he died, "that was what young men did back then." Raised in a house with a cook and chauffeur, Dad never learned the necessities behind maintaining a bachelor pad such as: cleaning, cooking, or doing laundry. During our last conversation, he informed me he married my mother mostly because she was beautiful and wouldn't let him have his way with her. Determined to make Else his wife, he chased her for the better half of their years together at the University of Michigan. Mother confided to me she fell in love with my father her freshman year but knew that in order to win his heart, she would have to play extremely hard to get. Her plan worked. They married on graduation day, June 13, 1952, staying together for over 62 years.

Graduating from the UofM with a journalism degree, Dad had two choices: either get shipped to Korea or join a new organization called the Central Intelligence Agency. He quickly chose the CIA desk job. Soon after marrying my mother, they set off for new beginnings, making their first home in Washington, D.C. Mother and Dad became parents with the arrivals of my sister Lisa in 1954 and brother Beau in 1957. From old photographs, it looks like they had a wonderful life including lovely homes complete with housekeepers and nannies, great friends, and lots of travel. Unfortunately, Dad told me his desk job bored him to tears and his long late-night work hours created added stress on the new family. He knew by the early 1960's he needed a career change.

His opportunity came when tragedy struck in 1961. His father, having battled cancer for the previous couple of years, died in March. After he passed, Dad made frequent trips home to Shelbyville to offer support to his newly widowed mother. During one of these trips back home, he and his brother Ben attended an auction for his hometown newspaper up for sale, *The Shelby Sentinel*. Having worked at the paper during summers between his school years, Dad dreamed of owning his own newspaper one day. With a bit of trepidation, Dad threw his hat in the ring to purchase the Sentinel, ultimately "winning" the prize. Winning is a word I use tongue in cheek. Bill Matthews bought himself a paper that spring but along with his purchase came crushing debt and years of hard work.

Also because of the purchase, they needed to move. My dad bought my newly widowed grandmother's house, and they left Washington to start anew in Dad's hometown. They moved into the "Big White House" in Shelbyville a few months before my arrival in November 1962. Working as a traditional stay at home wife, my mother spent nearly every day trying to keep up with the housework a gigantic six-bedroom, 80-year old house requires.

As a child, I remember my dad always being "at the office." In those days, putting out a weekly using antiquated printing equipment took hours of labor. But he was determined to support his family and worked long, hard days. He told me after surviving the grueling work for a few years, he knew he couldn't continue on the same path. Something had to change! A born innovator, Dad got busy figuring out a solution.

Almost overnight, my father and a few other newspapermen formed what would become Newspapers Inc. This new enterprise was a novel centralized printing facility that allowed multiple nearby newspapers to be printed in one location, saving participating newspapers time and money. Newspapers Inc. flourished. My dad enjoyed being the most successful financially he would ever be for the rest of his life (we of course didn't know this at the time). Dad sold his part of the business to a larger conglomerate after two years, staying employed with them for a while.

As it happened, it turned out to be a decidedly short while. Never a "company" man, Bill Matthews despised meetings and taking orders from anyone. He decided for his sanity's sake, he needed to forge a new path once more.

Perhaps being his most inventive, he published a separate newspaper in 1974 devoted entirely to the Cincinnati Reds baseball team. The first of its kind, Dad first called it *Pete Rose's Reds Alert*, highlighting all happenings surrounding the personal and professional lives of the players and management behind the Cincinnati Reds "Big Red Machine." Pete Rose's name was dropped soon after the paper's debut because of some dispute I was too young to comprehend. Nevertheless, the newspaper was "a hit" with Reds fans. It also helped that the Cincinnati Reds were "red hot" during this time period, winning the World Series in 1975 and '76. The magazine's flourishing subscription numbers enabled my parents to live "high on the hog." Clever Dad figured out a way to make a living attending Reds games, throwing parties attended by Reds players, and making a name for himself within sports journalism. For several years, he leased an apartment in Covington, Kentucky, across the river from Riverfront Stadium in downtown Cincinnati so he could be closer to the action. Those were heady years for my father. Not only did Dad have tickets for the best seats at the baseball games and access to players for frequent interviews, but he also received invitations to hang out with the players at the Reds' spring training base at Al Lopez field in Tampa, Florida.

Living a life befitting a movie star, Dad enjoyed buying custom suits and taking my mother on trips to Europe. In 1975, he purchased his dream car; a fire engine red Mercury Cougar XR7 coupe accented with white vinyl racing stripes running along the sides of its mammoth exterior. Being the only car like it in my hometown, this "ride" got noticed! From the first day Dad drove it home, my mother seemed to despise his vehicle, nicknaming it a "pimp mobile". Being only a girl of twelve, I wasn't too sure what she meant, but judging from her tone, I knew it couldn't be a compliment. For my mother, the car perhaps represented all the time Dad spent away from us.

Dad continued his close to Hollywood style of living for as long as he could, despite future dire consequences.

My father confided to me he "hung on to the *Reds Alert* too long." He could have sold it in 1977, making a nice profit for himself but chose to keep his paper one year too long. By the time he did sell it in 1978, he lost money on what had once been his goldmine. Reluctantly, he returned to more traditional newspaper publishing. Once more he worked long days, sitting in a traditional office of a small paper in the Louisville area. He continued to zip around in his beloved Cougar even as the odometer turned well past 150,000 miles. In the spring of 1980, I needed transportation of my own to get back and forth to school and to my job at McDonalds. Generously, Dad turned the Cougar keys over to me. Appreciating deeply having such a cool car, I tried to restore the car's faded red luster by giving "my" car its first wax job, ever. The white leather seats had cracked some but I didn't mind. I did, however, mind how expensive it was to fill up the huge tank. With the minimum wage at my McDonalds job being a measly $3.00 an hour and gasoline hovering around $1.00 a gallon, I highly doubt I ever said "fill 'er up" but I loved this car, possibly almost as much as my dad had when he first bought it.

After I left for college, Dad sold the Cougar. By this time, it had been driven over 205,000 miles. For a few years, I'd see other Cougars of the same make and color but by the late 1990s, the sighting of a mid-'70s two-door Cougar was rare, especially red ones.

The lean years of the late '70s into the 1980s helped my father master the concept of making lemonade out of lemons, even when he had little juice. Over the next two decades, he continued to publish all kinds of newspapers, magazines, and Kentucky Visitors guides before finally moving into books. He spent a lot of time on the road but otherwise, he was usually found at his office at 612 East 6th Street in downtown Shelbyville, synonymous with his idea of being "at home".

After my mother died, Dad spent as much time as possible at his humble workplace. Literally filled with newspapers and magazines he had published over the years; the place was a mess. My dad, fancying himself a collector, never seemed to mind all the accumulation. Fortunately, his house stayed clean because his kind housekeeper Shelley, who had been with my parents for years, stayed on to help Dad. I'm pretty sure that going into his 86th year, he had rarely used a washing machine or a floor mop. He proved to be a decent cook; however, he never understood that pots and pans don't clean themselves.

His business partner, Mae, was largely responsible for Dad's newspaper ventures being so successful. Masterful with details, Mae helped make sure Dad's publications were printed by their deadlines and that the financials were kept in good and orderly shape. Previously, these particulars had been rather elusive for my father.

Mae and my dad had known each other for decades. By this time, she'd been a widow for years. It
seemed natural, at least to me, that they could enjoy
each other's company more and more after my mother
died. None of us kids lived close enough to help Dad
out on a daily basis so we felt grateful that Dad and
Mae had each other. Nine months after my mother's
death, Dad decided to move out of the family home
and move in with Mae. They talked about marriage.
I felt particularly happy for them both because they
seemed to enjoy each other's company so darn much.

In the fall of 2016, we siblings showed up to clear
out the house and attend settlement after Dad sold
his home. With Dad choosing not to keep much, we
siblings rented our own moving trucks to haul piles
of stuff and furniture back to our respective homes.
Working non-stop, we siblings and spouses helped
load each other's vans while occasionally sharing
funny stories from our childhoods. During this whole
weekend of busy activity, I noticed with concern,
my Dad appeared uncharacteristically quiet. More
ominously, he sat for the most part of each day in
an antique Victorian chair he didn't even like. Usually, he loved sharing stories attached to the various
treasures accumulated over the years. Uncharacteristically, he barely said a word all weekend.

My gut told me Dad wasn't feeling well. Despite
our attempts to engage him he continued to sit and
observe for most of the weekend. Dad's face also
appeared almost gray. When he did walk around the

house, he seemed to get short of breath more easily than usual. Of course, when I asked him if he was feeling OK, he always answered, "Yes, just fine." He couldn't convince me though. I was pretty sure his quiet mood wasn't related to the selling of the house or this move being "the end of an era," as he liked to quip whenever a big change within the family happened.

After the house sale was final on Monday morning Sept 26, 2016, Dad walked me to the moving van outside the law office where Pete was waiting for me. I asked Dad once more, after noticing he still didn't appear well, "Are you sure you are ok?"

"Yes Ellie Belle, I'm fine." Unconvinced, I said while hopping into the front seat of the van, "I'll call you tomorrow. Please go get checked out if you feel any worse, ok?"

"I will, I will," he said without conviction before waving goodbye as we pulled away.

After Pete and I made it back safely to Pennsylvania, Dad and I spoke daily. He didn't mention his health although I could perceive by his weak voice that his condition hadn't gotten any better. Two weeks later, on Henrik's 23rd birthday (and the first anniversary of my mother's death), Dad finally phoned me with a report on his health. He was calling from a hospital bed and the news wasn't good.

Diagnosed with myelodysplasia, Dad called to say he already felt much better after receiving multiple blood transfusions. All his symptoms of fatigue, shortness of breath, poor color and lack of energy were related to his bone marrow not functioning normally any longer. The cause wasn't exactly known. In the following weeks, he received many more transfusions though they only offered limited relief. By the winter months of 2017, my dad knew his days were numbered. He no longer talked about marrying Mae nor planned that second cross country train trip he had wanted to do so much. One day I knew it had become dire. During our conversation he confided, "I've stopped driving." My heart seized a bit upon his telling me this news. My dad enjoyed driving more than most any other activity. Looking back, it is easy to see how each of his cars reflected how things were going for him, emotionally and financially.

For instance, during those prosperous years of the early '70s, Dad drove a 1971 Mercury Marquis (all six of us fit into that boat), followed by his favorite of all time, the big red Cougar. After the collapse of his Reds venture, he drove a modest Volkswagen Golf which leaked oil constantly. In the 1990s, with his financial picture still on the slim side, he putted around in a Dodge Neon he affectionately called "The Little Green Streak". When the little car started literally to shake, Pete and I gifted him our well-used 1989 Ford Taurus wagon followed by our second Taurus wagon we lent him until Phil needed his own transportation in college. Fortunately, by this time, Dad's newspaper businesses had improved financially. He purchased a Ford Edge which proved to be reliable transportation for thousands of miles of sales calls. Of all of these automobiles however, he told me his favorite remained his 1975 red Cougar. Together, the car and the man had been a real pair.

So the news of him not driving hit me hard, but because I had been grounded in airports by bad weather too many times in the previous years, I didn't fly to Kentucky during the winter of 2017. Dad and I did talk though, every day, sometimes twice a day. No matter how rough his medical treatments made him feel, he never complained to me. He even somehow found the energy to publish one last magazine he had promised to complete by mid-spring.

Incredibly, in late March, in what truly was the twilight of his life, he received the best phone call of his life. He had waited almost a lifetime for this news. I'll never forget our conversation.

"Ellie Belle?" my dad said when I answered the phone at home in Pennsylvania. I could tell something big was up.

"Hey dad, what's going on?"

With more excitement than I had heard from him in a while, he said, "I got a big phone call today. I got news, big news."

"OK—I'm ready."

Then with as much enthusiasm as he could muster, he announced, "I've been selected into the Kentucky Journalism Hall of Fame."

Tears immediately filled my eyes. I knew this award was an honor he had secretly been hoping for his entire career as a newspaperman.

"Oh Daddy! That's wonderful! I'm so happy for you! Oh, my goodness, you must be so thrilled!"

Dad went on to tell me about the awards reception being held in late April. In fact, he already had composed a list of guests whom he wanted to invite to the ceremony. I had never heard him so excited. Offering more congratulatory remarks, I hung up from our conversation hoping he would live long enough to make it to his induction personally.

I will never forget the last time I visited my father. When I flew down to see him the third week of April 2017, I expected the worst. However, when I walked into the living room to find him sitting on the sofa, my fears were calmed. I found my dad sitting up in his favorite robe with the cutest grin on his face. As I walked into the room, he greeted me with a delightful, "Hello Ellie Belle."

Knowing this could be the last conversation we would have in person, we got busy covering any and all topics.

What does one talk about during last conversations? We covered the gamut. He reviewed his marriage, career, and his hopes for my sons, finally sharing some last revelations I had no previous knowledge about. He did most of the talking. I tried committing everything to memory so I'd never forget our last time together. As the afternoon progressed, he became increasingly short of breath but he didn't want to stop. Suddenly, much to my dismay, I held my own breath as I witnessed a scary event happening right before my eyes.

In the middle of telling me another one of his stories, Dad's speech suddenly became garbled. Mid-sentence he vacantly stared ahead, eyes and mouth open.

"Oh God. Dad's having a stroke."

I sat and looked at him hoping and praying he would come out of whatever was happening to him quickly. My mind was a flurry of questions: "Do I call an ambulance?" "What if he stops breathing?" "What if he collapses right here on the sofa?"

I remembered Dad had made it clear in his own Five Wishes living will he did not want heroic measures taken if he should stop breathing or his heart stopped beating. But witnessing him having an apparent stroke firsthand put me into a bit of a panic. I didn't want to lose my dad at that moment.

And then, as suddenly as it began, his symptoms improved rapidly. After 30 seconds or so, Dad's speech returned to normal and he was able to lift his arms and look at me again. Like an old Victrola record player which had run down, he suddenly came back to life as if an imaginary crank wound him back to normal.

Looking straight at me, Dad asked, "Did you notice that?" "I think I just had some kind of a stroke."

"Yep, Dad, I did see that." "Are you OK?" He nodded his head affirming he was apparently "OK."

Without another word about the incident, he continued on, telling me the last of all the things he wanted me to know. Some of his information did truly surprise me but I listened, loving him all the more. We had three precious hours of solid conversation before stopping for dinner. Ever mindful of his precarious health, we both felt so lucky to have this time alone together.

Since his birthday was the next week, I gave him his card and gift. I stayed as long as possible before kissing my dad on his head telling him one more time how lucky I felt to have him for a father. He told me he loved me too before saying "I'll see you in the next world Ellie Belle." During the afternoon, I brought up signs and the possibility he might send one, but he didn't say too much about this idea. I'm sure he had other things on his mind.

One such thing being his induction into the Kentucky Journalism Hall of Fame. With my brothers Beau and Bland's help, he attended in a wheelchair; too weak to walk on his own. He somehow found the strength to give a short acceptance speech. Sadly, the occasion turned out to be his last public appearance.

He passed three weeks later in hospice care, on May 13, 2017, with Mae at his side.

Dad desired a simple memorial service, which was held in late May. Of course, my father had carefully orchestrated the entire thing before he became too ill. Before we siblings returned home, we had a bit of business to discuss. While we had dispersed most of his possessions the previous fall, a few items remained that he had refused to part with after selling his home. Now we needed to figure out what to do with it all.

In September 2017, my siblings and I made arrangements to gather once again to meet at Mae's garage to divide up the books and multiple boxes of Dad's "treasures." Filling at least fifteen plastic tubs, his most cherished belongings ranged from sports figures bobbleheads, toy planes, cars and trucks, and a few mysterious looking coin collections. I flew back to Kentucky staying this time with my cousin Blair and her husband Hunter in Louisville, renting a car for the meet up the following day with my two brothers. Fortunately, the weather cooperated. My drive from the city to the country didn't take long; 20 miles or so of interstate before the ten miles of country roads leading to the tiny town of New Castle, Kentucky, population a bit over 900.

To my delight it was a glorious day for a drive.

After exiting the freeway, I drove slowly preparing soon for the next stop sign seen yards ahead. This is a tranquil and less traveled part of our world. For all the times I had turned at this particular exit, I might have seen ten other cars pass by going the other way toward the interstate entrance. As I neared the second stop sign, something made me notice the car parked at the corner of the intersection. Feeling compelled to look more closely, I spotted a moss colored late model vehicle sitting by itself with a small "For Sale" sign in its window. In all the times I had stopped at this spot, not once to my recollection had there ever been a vehicle of any sort sitting at this particular quiet corner.

As I rolled to my stop, I peered intently to get a better look at the vehicle. The car's long hood looked ten feet long, the coupe doors were massive, and it had the familiar and distinctive front grill that seemed to say, "I'm an old, but in obviously good condition "pimp mobile." My mouth dropped open when it dawned on me this car was no other than a mid-1970s vintage Mercury Cougar. Although not exactly the same, the front grill looked identical to the car we both had loved so much, further convincing me the model years had to be close.

Dumbfounded, I sat in my own rental car staring for a while. Finally, proceeding on to Mae's house, I grinned all the rest of the way there feeling certain I had received my sign from my dad.

Both brothers arrived shortly after me. We immediately set upon our task of clearing out the last of my dad's worldly possessions (besides a few hundred leftover books from all his enterprises). The time flew with only a couple of folks stopping to ask, "Y'all having a yard sale?"

When almost finished, I asked my brother Bland, "Did you notice anything unusual on the drive out?"

Without blinking he said, "You mean the car?"

"Yeah, the car," I said laughing. "That car had to be dad's sign letting us know he's with us today." Expectantly, I watched for their reaction to my statement. Neither brother said much, which was understandable given they didn't know any details of my previous experiences with receiving signs. We finished our clean up later in the afternoon before leaving in our separate cars. I eagerly drove back toward Louisville wanting another look at the car "For Sale."

Interestingly, the Cougar wasn't there when I returned to the intersection. I never saw another one until recently, in September, 2020.

After a sleepless night worrying about the final details I needed to complete before sending this book to the printer, I felt I desperately needed exercise and a change of scenery. Henrik was visiting from New Hampshire for the week and made sure he took some time off for pandemic-safe outings. Being a beautiful day, we put masks in our pocket and drove into Philadelphia. We enjoyed a delightful afternoon covering over four miles of city blocks before returning to our car parked near the Delaware River.

As we neared one of the many intersections on the city boulevard, a gleaming all-white 1975 Mercury Cougar raced by us. The car didn't look a day old. Six blocks later, we saw parked, in mint condition, a fire engine red 1975 Ford Thunderbird with a white vinyl roof and racing stripes.

Pete calls our seeing them "coincidences".

Perhaps.

I like to think of them as the messages of encouragement I needed at the time.

Thanks, Dad.

CHAPTER 11

The Last Hand

All of the signs seemingly meant for me occurred without warning or request. I never said, "If you are here Mother, send me a sign!" As with prayer, one doesn't know when prayers are going to be answered. Instead, it is more important to keep an open mind and be ready for the answer, regardless of whether or not it's what we requested. A friend of mine, James, made a profound statement after hearing this particular passage. He responded, "Everything happens for a reason. We don't sometimes understand it at the moment."

And so, it would seem the same with signs. In conclusion, allow me to share a follow up story from the ones about my sister Lisa and our father. It suggests we can be sent continuing messages—if and when we keep our eyes and mind open.

On a gorgeous fall afternoon of 2018, Pete suggested we go for a walk in the neighborhood. Autumn is a particularly spectacular time of year in Wallingford. The leaves had turned their various colors of orange, yellow and red and many leaf piles sat ready for pick up along our street. Pete had added several of his own a few yards past the end of our driveway.

As we turned the corner to begin our walk, Pete noticed "trash" lying on top of one of the leaf piles. Bending to pick it up, he noticed right away this "litter" was actually two playing cards.

He and I looked around for the rest of the deck, but no, we only found these two cards. It seemed odd to find random playing cards alongside the road. I placed them in my pocket after glancing at them for a second. "I'll throw them out when we get back."

I'm not sure what made me stop and look at them again more closely; maybe the sheer oddness of finding two playing cards lying alone on the piles of leaves. Neighborhood kids sometimes throw out bottles, drink containers, or empty packs of cigarettes but we'd never found playing cards before.

And then, of course, I got to thinking these weren't merely playing cards but maybe something else.

Within minutes I had my answer. Instead of picking up trash, I apparently picked up two "greeting cards" from my deceased sister Lisa.

You see, I had first picked up a five and then a four of diamonds–"54". The day of this walk was October 18th, what would have been my sister's 64th birthday had she been alive. She was born in 1954.

I told Pete about my connecting the two cards with my sister's birth year. Pete and I smiled and looked up toward heaven wishing her a happy birthday. I still keep the "greeting" cards on my bulletin board to remind me of my sister every time I notice them.

Oddly enough, on the following day, Pete found one more card on a different but nearby leaf pile: the Ace of Diamonds.

Feeling certain this particular card had to be a related sign to the other two cards, I kept it for a while, trying to figure out its meaning.

Three months went by before the light bulb went off. When it did, I quickly found Pete.

My dad loved attending murder mystery weekends at hotels over the years. Possibly finding it amusing to put his old CIA skills to use, he always tried to convince the other players he was the murderer, despite this never being the case.

He always used the same alias, B.B. Diamond.

And this third card? It appeared to be from the same apparent deck as the "5" and "4" (both diamonds as well). With the connection still too loose, I examined the playing cards more closely on both sides. Finally, it all made sense.

There, on the back of each card are two bicy-clists—the signature emblem for Bicycle brand playing cards.

Bicycle brand "BB" Ace of Diamonds—a.k.a.—B.B. Diamond, my father's best loved alias.

Thinking about the two of them sending me greeting cards still makes me chuckle today. No tell-ing what those two are cooking up to send next. I'm keeping my eyes and mind open in the meantime.

CHAPTER 12

A Sign in Memoriam

In the Memory of Jay Zook
April 10, 1952—April 20, 2020

"Be at peace dear friend. I'm so sorry
I didn't get to say good-bye"

E nough already.
It was time to get serious about figuring out what to do with all these stories about my receiving apparent signs.

In the fall of 2017, I seriously began to organize my notes. Slowly, something kind of resembling a cohesive story began taking shape loosely tying the received "signs" together.

A year later, my first attempt turned out to be more or less a 30,000 word "rough" draft. A *really* rough draft. Feeling a bit lost, I knew I needed to "hear" my stories by reading them aloud to someone. Getting some much-needed feedback seemed like a good idea too. After all, my degree is in nursing, not non-fiction writing. Perhaps this was a silly endeavor, yet, something continued to compel me to keep at it.

In the fall of 2018, I learned my dear friend Jay, the former Assistant Manager at the Brandywine Regional Airport, was recuperating at a nearby rehabilitation center after suffering severe injuries from a previous fall. Jay and I became instant good friends during the two years Phil was flying at Brandywine as he was either at the desk or out fueling planes when I drove Phil to the airport for his lessons with Hagan. Since I knew his beloved brother (and best friend) Frank, had died fairly recently leaving Jay with little family in the area, Pete and I paid him a visit days before Christmas. Much to Jay's delight, Pete disguised a few beers as Christmas gifts for them to enjoy together. I hadn't seen my dear friend in a long while and I was dismayed how thin and frail he looked. Sadly, he seriously doubted he would ever be well enough to leave his current living situation. He was only 66 years old but his continuing health problems were inhibiting him from making a full recovery. Jay's fall might have shattered his bones but obviously not his mind or his fun-loving spirit. He was so upbeat during our holiday visit. He said something about being bored to tears at times but on this lovely day together, we laughed a lot.

Like before, way back when.

After Pete's and my visit, I returned to check on Jay by myself during the winter of 2019. He filled me in on his close encounter with death after his horrible fall. He further explained that what I saw on his side of the semi-private room was all he had left in the world. Nothing from his stash of wonderful aviation memorabilia he had collected over his lifetime appeared to be anywhere. When I asked him about his collection, he responded, "Oh, it's long gone. It all had to be sold." I felt so sad.

Eventually I got around to asking him to be my audience. "Hey, I'm trying to write a book about getting "signs" from people who have died. Yea, I know it sounds crazy. But, what would you think about listening to some of the stories? I'd love your opinion on whether or not to continue with this project." He laughed before responding, "Sure," without asking any details. Of course, it was obvious to both of us that he was more or less a "captive but willing audience" when he graciously accepted.

So, beginning in the spring of 2019, I stopped by with my Chromebook in hand to begin reading some of my stories to Jay while he sat a few feet away in his wheelchair. I noticed by the third visit he had put on some much-needed weight giving him a much healthier appearance.

He proved to be an enormous help to me. In places where I used too many medical terms, he commented, "Use words everyone can understand."

In more than one instance he exclaimed, "Ugh, that's too graphic. Don't get so grizzly." With his encouragement spurring me on, I immediately re-wrote several chapters so my words didn't make readers squirm from the gory details which can sometimes occur during end of life situations.

Mostly though, Jay supported my storytelling by expressing a real interest in the stories and making me feel that maybe I could write a real book of sorts. We never talked about signs between ourselves. Instead, we always made plans for our next visit.

I last saw my friend Jay in person on his 67th birthday on April 10, 2019. Two other lady friends from his "old days" joined me for a couple of hours of reminiscing. He remained in his wheelchair as we gathered around a table in the lobby of the rehab center. He appeared even stronger than when we visited last. My photos from that day are evidence of his obvious pleasure at being surrounded by balloons, at least two birthday cakes, and a basket of candy treats. And the stories these ladies shared—oh, the stories!

It turns out Jay had quite the colorful past. It was especially fun hearing about his motorcycle riding days and in particular the many wild ski weekends spent with friends back in the 1970s. And of course, he talked about his passion; flying. By this time, he knew his days in a cockpit were over but he hoped soon he could get his hands strong enough to use the joy stick for the flight simulator loaded into his laptop.

Sadly, I never saw Jay again. Time got away from me in the fall of 2019. We did wish each other Merry Christmas online. He later responded via Facebook Messenger to my greetings from Melbourne, Australia, in January 2020 with, "Watch out for the Tazmanian Devils!! Safe travels, Love, JBird." I certainly meant to stop by to see him once my spring job near his facility resumed. Since I had already made the changes to my book he had suggested, I thought maybe he wouldn't mind listening to the reworked passages?

Then, in mid-March, my marketing job came to an abrupt halt. In fact, much of the world came to a stop. With blinding speed, a new virus called Covid-19 was making people severely ill and all too often causing death. We healthcare workers found ourselves in the midst of a pandemic with possible horrendous consequences for so many, particularly the aged and those with weak immune systems like Jay.

I was no longer welcome to do my marketing visits with patients at nearby dialysis centers. By the end of March, those of us in the Philadelphia area were ordered to "Stay at Home." Having no previous experience with pandemics, I found this period of time the most frightening I've ever experienced. Making the situation even more surreal and scary, many of my friends were in the particular age group designated to be more "at risk." Frighteningly, we didn't know what was going to happen (and presently in July 2020, it appears we still don't).

With so much time on my hands, I got busy redis-covering a type of old-fashioned correspondence, the sending of cards and letters. Remembering Jay had a birthday on April 10th, I sent him a card wishing him a "Happy Birthday." I found it a bit ominous I didn't hear from him via Messenger during the week but figured I'd reach out again soon.

Each passing 24 hours seemed like a true "Ground Hog Day." On Thursday morning, April 23, Pete and I looked at each other wondering again how to spend yet one more day at home on lockdown. So far, we had cleaned every cupboard and closet in the house. I had written more letters to friends and relatives than I had in the past ten years. Pete got so desperate for something to do, he cleaned out the shed he hadn't thoroughly gone through in over two decades. Rather languidly, I suggested we tackle the attic. "Let's pull down all the boxes not related to Christmas and go through them." It sounded like a dirty, messy ordeal. But before I could finish my morning sixth cup of coffee, Pete had already lowered the attic stairs, wait-ing to pass down the first of many boxes representing years of accumulation.

Many of these cardboard boxes and plastic tubs were full of keepsakes from the boys' youngest years. As a new mother, I apparently kept every scrap of artwork Phil produced from the ages of two to four.

As a not so new mother after Henrik's arrival, I discovered I hadn't kept nearly the same amount of "works of art" for either boy. Nevertheless, I managed to combine six boxes of "memories" into one for each son. What a sense of accomplishment!

I found two boxes filled with stuffed animals. Again, more consolidation! This cleaning out the attic sure was proving productive.

Next, I found a big tub filled with toy models, action figures, beat up Hot Wheels cars, and even an old snake skin. This particular tub had once belonged to Phil. Pulling out each item filled my head with so many memories.

Lastly, I pulled out a clear plastic bag filled with small metal planes. They were from the collection Phil used to create his busy airports as a boy. Feeling increasingly nostalgic, I took each one out of the well-worn bag and lined them up as Phil once did during so many play times in our family room. I felt remorseful I hadn't kept at least one of his cardboard airport layouts. Phil put so much effort into making each appear authentic with crisscrossing runways, a tower, and of course a bustling terminal. No way could I dispose of any of these toy planes, though many of them had chipped paint or slightly bent wings from years of play. I took a photo of them all lined up on the carpet thinking that maybe Phil would have a little pilot of his own one day who would enjoy them.

With the planes still sitting where I "parked" them, I took a break to have lunch and check my phone for messages.

My friend, Rosalie, whose husband flies his own plane in and out of the Brandywine Regional Airport had left me a message. Sadly, I learned that Jay had passed three days before. My mouth fell open. This was such unexpected news.

While still trying to fully comprehend what I was reading, my eyes kept focusing on Phil's plane collection still on the carpeted "tarmac."

I read more fully the details regarding Jay's death, learning Jay had died of complications related to Covid-19.

I immediately thought, "How odd to receive word about Jay so soon after literally 'playing' with Phil's childhood airplane collection." Looking at Phil's planes while fully grasping Jay had lost his life to the same virus that kept us at home cleaning out attics and closets made me grieve deeply for my kind and supportive friend. Writing this months later, I still lament the fact I can't joke around with Jay online any longer. On a positive note, I know he is most certainly in a much better place. Undoubtedly, he is flying his beloved WWII fighter planes somewhere in the great beyond.

I still believe those little planes of Phil's served as both a reminder of Jay and a special sign he is at peace. I smile while thinking of him being once again in good health sharing funny jokes in the great "airport" in the sky.

Jay's obituary reads that his "service and interment" were private. Because of the continuing potential harm of the Covid-19, larger gatherings are still prohibited in Pennsylvania. I am so sorry I have not had the opportunity to properly say goodbye to my dear friend. This chapter is written in your memory, Jbird. You will be missed and always remembered.

There is a kind of principle of the sky
A spirit of flight that calls
to certain among mankind
as the wilderness calls to some
And the sea, to others

—Richard Bach

CHAPTER 13

In the Absence of Faith

Not long ago, I spoke with a woman who began telling me about her brother whom she took care of before he died from a neurologic disease. He moved in with her when he could no longer take care of himself. They spent quality time together before his death. She told me that right before he died, she brought up the notion of his sending her a sign from the afterlife. After consideration, he told her he would come back as an owl.

At the time of our chat, he had already been deceased for many months.

"Have you seen any owls?" I asked her.

"No, I haven't seen any owls," she said, with disappointment in her voice.

"Hmmm, that's a shame," I said, sad for her she hadn't gotten her "sign" from her brother. After mulling this story over, I had to ask her, "Did your brother have faith?"

Quickly, she replied, "No. He didn't. He was an atheist. Do you think that's why I haven't gotten a sign?"

"I'm not sure," was all I could say. Who am I to make such a determination? It did give us both reason to contemplate fully the question, "Can one send and receive signs when there is no faith in a higher being?"

My personal belief in God, an afterlife and "signs" is surrounded by a certain mystery where there can be no proof. Possibly, these signs only make themselves known when there is faith and hope and of course, love.

Signs—comforting messages, or mere coincidences? I prefer to think of them as spiritual links between all of us here on earth and those in the next realm. While I certainly will never embrace death, these experiences have helped me face my own demise with a lot less fear.

There's only one question that still stumps me.

What will my sign be?

What will be yours?

ACKNOWLEDGEMENTS

This book has been a work in progress for many years. I wish to convey a huge "thank-you" to the many friends and relatives who have been so supportive to me during the writing and publishing process. In addition, I have some folks I would like to especially acknowledge. They include my father William E. Matthews, Dr. Chad Brecher, James Gerber, Dawn Craigie, and my brother, Beau Matthews. Instead of laughing, my older brother shared with me his own "signs" he feels he has received. A note of appreciation goes to Ryan Schurman and Mary Ann Hellinghausen who encouraged me in the beginning to keep writing. Of course, a special tribute goes to the memory of Jay Zook, who patiently listened and helped me make much needed revisions. To my sons, Phil and Henrik, thank you for letting me share some of my writing during the rainy days of our recent family vacation. Your feedback truly reshaped the beginning of my story.

A special remark of gratitude goes to my supportive husband, Pete, who gave me the space and time to finally finish this book. It has been a long time in the making.

Thank you to Rosalie Phipps for creating the incredible oil painting of a moth which adorns my cover and to her husband, Craig Stock, for his support and time spent proofreading.

Finally, my gratitude goes to Sarah Maddack (she was responsible for the "out of the blue" phone call described in the introduction), to my writing coach Scott Allan who kept me on track and finally, to my editor, Katie Chambers, who helped improve my rusty writing skills enormously.

AUTHOR BIO

A native of Shelbyville, Kentucky, Ellen Matthews Oetinger graduated from Western Kentucky University in 1985 with an Associate's Degree in Nursing, later earning her Bachelor's Degree in Nursing from Immaculata University in 2012. The mother of two grown sons, Ellen resides outside of Philadelphia, Pennsylvania, with her husband Pete.